Negotiating with Borderline Personality

A Lawyer looks at Borderline Personality Disorder

Thomas Mengert, J.D.

KITSAP
PUBLISHING

KITSAP PUBLISHING

Negotiating with Borderline Personality
A Lawyer looks at Borderline Personality Disorder
First edition, published 2023

By Thomas Mengert, J.D.
Cover design: Kitsap Publishing
Cover art: www.istockphoto.com, iStock_000050131938

ISBN-13: 978-1-942661-27-6

Published by Kitsap Publishing
P.O. Box 572
Poulsbo, WA 98370
www.KitsapPublishing.com

Epigraph

Those which are jealous, most part, if they be not otherwise relieved, proceed from suspicion to hatred, from hatred to frenzy, madness, injury, murder and despair. A plague by whose most damnable effect divers in deep despair to die have sought, by which a man to madness near is brought, as well with causeless as with just suspect. In their madness many times they make away themselves and others. Which induceth Cyprian to call it, Foecundam et multiplicem perniciem, fontem cladium et seminarium delictorum, a fruitful mischief, the seminary of offences, and fountain of murders. Tragical examples are too common in this kind both new and old in all ages.

Suspicion and jealousy are general symptoms: they are commonly distrustful, apt to mistake, and amplify, facile irascibiles, testy, pettish, peevish, and ready to snarl upon every small occasion, and without a cause. If they speak in jest, he takes it in good earnest. If they be not saluted, invited, consulted with, called to counsel, &c., or that any respect, small compliment, or ceremony be omitted, they think themselves neglected, and contemned; for a time that tortures them. If two talk together, discourse, whisper, jest, or tell a tale in general, he thinks presently they mean him, applies all to himself. Or if they talk with him, he is ready to misconstrue every word they speak, and interpret it to the worst; he cannot endure any man to look steadily on him, speak to him almost, laugh, jest, or be familiar, or hem, or point, cough, or spit, or make a noise sometimes, &c. He thinks they laugh or point at him, or do it in disgrace of him, circumvent him, contemn him; every man looks at him, he is pale, red, sweats for fear and anger, lest somebody should observe him. He works upon it, and long after this false conceit of an abuse troubles him. Montanus gives instance in a melancholy Jew, that was so waspish and suspicious that no man could tell how to carry himself in his company.

Inconstant they are in all their actions, vertiginous, restless, unapt to resolve of any business, they will and will not, persuaded to and fro upon every small occasion, or word spoken: and yet if once they be resolved, obstinate, hard to be reconciled. If they abhor, dislike, or distaste, once settled, though to the better by odds, by no counsel, or persuasion, to be removed, yet in most things wavering, irresolute, unable to deliberate through fear. Now prodigal, and then covetous, they do, and by-and-by repent them of that which they have done, so that both ways they are troubled, whether they do or do not, want or have, hit or miss, disquieted of all hands, soon weary, and still seeking change, restless, I say, fickle, fugitive, they may not abide to tarry in one place long.

Extreme passionate, and what they desire, they do most furiously seek; anxious ever, and very solicitous, distrustful, and timorous, envious, malicious, profuse one while, sparing another, but most part covetous, muttering, repining, discontent, and still complaining, grudging, peevish, prone to revenge, soon troubled, and most violent in all their imaginations, not affable in speech, or apt to vulgar compliment, but surly, dull, sad, austere; still, very intent, and as Albertus Durer paints melancholy, like a sad woman leaning on her arm with fixed looks, neglected habit, &c., held therefore by some proud, soft, sottish, or half-mad, as the Abderites esteemed of Democritus: and yet of a deep reach, excellent apprehension, judicious, wise, and witty: for I am of that nobleman's mind, Melancholy advanceth men's conceits, more than any humour whatsoever, improves their meditations more than any strong drink or sack.

They are of profound judgment in some things, although in others they count honesty dishonesty, friends as enemies, they will abuse their best friends, and dare not offend their enemies. Cowards most part loath to offend, and if they chance to overshoot themselves in word or deed: or any small business or circumstance be omitted, forgotten, they are miserably tormented, and frame a thousand dangers and inconveniences to themselves if once they conceit it: overjoyed with every good rumor, tale, or prosperous event, transported beyond themselves: with every small cross again, bad news, misconceived injury, loss, danger, afflicted beyond measure, in great agony, perplexed, dejected, astonished, impatient, utterly undone: fearful, suspicious of all.

Inveterate Melancholy, howsoever it may seem to be a continuate, inexorable disease, hard to be cured, accompanying them to their graves, most part, as Montanus observes, yet many times it may be helped, even that which is most violent, or at least, according to the same author, it may be mitigated and much eased. It may be hard to cure, but not impossible for him that is most grievously affected, if he but willing to be helped.

Being extracts from: "The Anatomy of Melancholy
Written in the 17th Century by Robert Burton

Table of Contents

Why This Book Was Written

This book was written at the same time that I was engaged in writing "Dean Langdell Is Dead" a book about the changes that have occurred in the practice of law and the resulting necessity for extensive reforms in the legal system. There was a time when to be a Counselor at Law laid as much emphasis upon the title of counselor as upon the role of legal technician. Lawyers were the last remaining generalists, persons who might use their unique skills to probe many aspects of the human equation and generally guide persons who found themselves in perplexing circumstances towards wise solutions to their problems.

Recent changes, many of them driven by technology and globalization, have called into question the role of the attorney in providing what are now being generically termed "legal services" rather than "lawyer services." The implication is that the role of an attorney may in many instances be assumed by others who have not been trained in the law and awarded a degree of Juris Doctor (doctor of jurisprudence) and have passed a State Bar Examination before being given a license to practice law. It is assumed by many that lawyers should be relegated to one of two positions that do not square with the traditional concepts of their role in society:

1. That of specialists who can be dispensed with except when an extremely complicated legal question arises;

2. That of litigators whose sole business should be representing clients before courts of law.

All other legal functions are assumed to be increasingly fungible and capable of being farmed out as it were to legal process outsources or to other professions. Never has the multiplex role of the trained lawyer been so diminished in the public view. It therefore seemed a propitious time to take a broader view of the lawyer function and to reinstate our role as counselors not simply to clients in the course of active practice but to the public at large. The contribution of lawyers to the culture of the times may far exceed their more specific functions. Lawyers can provide a unique perspective and an analytic habit of mind that is unique to their training. It is from this perspective that the present book was written.

Persons with BPD may encounter the legal system at many levels, in family law hearings such as divorce or child custody, in cases involving various criminal infractions, or in cases involving bankruptcy, hospitalization, and other instances where the many unfortunate life events that flow from their illness may lead persons with BPD to encounter the legal system. These are too diverse to be discussed here. Instead I hope to demonstrate a legal habit of mind to attempt to elucidate the condition of BPD itself rather than to explore its multiple manifestations and consequences.

Is BPD an illness or a global if maladjusted way of approaching all experiences in the life of the Borderline? Even the word illness implies that an antecedent medical model is the sole way of looking at BPD. The very concept of a personality disorder is an extension of psychology into making value judgments as to character. Judgments such as these were not traditionally within the ambit of medicine or even of psychology. They were more often seen as questions of ethics, religion, philosophy, or literature. Our era is increasingly a battleground waged among the various professions to demonstrate that a given subject is within its jurisdiction. The phenomenon of professional augmentation or diminishment has hitherto been inadequately noticed.

If the realm of the exclusive competence of lawyers may be questioned in various areas as now appears to be the case it seems no less fair to ask if the customary modes of thought of an attorney might be of use in the realm traditionally assigned to psychology. If BPD is approached from the standpoint of the way that lawyers are trained to look at things, perhaps new insights might emerge.

Among these habits of the law is the question of the obligation to negotiate in good faith. Our world depends upon the existence of a certain level of basic trust in other people. This existential trust is increasingly rare among us. Many people in America apparently feel that they must arm themselves merely to preserve their life, property, and well-being. This indicates that we as a nation may have passed beyond civilization into a state of collective moral chaos. The same is true for individuals. The personality disorders whether anti-social, narcissistic, schizotypal, histrionic, or borderline disrupt normal social functioning and interfere with daily living and the reliability that we must place upon each other as we interact in a complex world. This failure to trust results in disappointed hopes, social friction, and sooner or later implicates the laws. It may not be too much to say that most litigation follows as frequently from the results of various personality disorders as from good-faith mistakes or conflicting interests.

For these reasons I have attempted to write what I hope will be received as a sympathetic effort to portray the life dilemmas that make a diagnosis of BPD so painful to all involved and to suggest that the humble criteria of legal contractual concepts and principles might point to a new way of proceeding through the multiple transactions that constitute daily living in our stressful and changing world for all who must deal in the ordinary course of events with persons who manifest symptoms of BPD.

In doing this I am simultaneously arguing for an expanded area of relevance for what has been called the statesman ideal as a measuring standard of the attorney function which includes evaluating social norms even when these are not reduced to statutory form or case law and to provide wise counsel for the different courses of social action that may be pursued to avoid unnecessary conflicts and wasted resources. This expansive and almost philosophical role was once considered natural for lawyers to assume in discussing diverse issues of social concern and it may be time to reclaim this right to bear testimony from the social sciences by efforts as small as this present contribution.

To be a lawyer once meant far more than merely hanging up one's shingle to practice law. Lawyers were also students of life and scrutinizers of human nature. The domain of the scholar of letters and of the laws was at one time as pragmatic, relevant, and respected as that of those professions with more restrictive subject matter credentials. The parameters of inquiry should be more universal it seems to me and who may say from whence new insights may proceed even in highly specific areas. It is in this spirit that the present volume has been written. By seeing BPD from a more oblique point of view perhaps new insights may appear that may guide practitioners as they pursue their more specialized inquiries into this puzzling condition.

Disclaimers

Having just proclaimed so much latitude as regards a right of inquiry this disclaimer is meant to restrict its applicability in the practical order. It is important that the readers of this book understand that it is an impressionistic study written by an attorney and not as an attorney. The distinction is critical: no legal advice or therapeutic treatment manual or professional expertise is being offered in this book.

This book is also not to be used as if its author is a practicing psychotherapist, psychologist, or psychiatrist. The book must stand on its own as a testimony to my own opinions, my own reading of BPD. Whatever value and validation the views expressed here may have must be derived from the reader's inner assent because they resonate with the experience of the reader. The perspective used here to approach BPD is an informed one but one that is freed from the usual constraints imposed by strict scholarship. For this reason footnotes and a list of the books that I have consulted before and during its composition have not been included so as not to mislead the reader regarding the reliability or accuracy of the synthesis presented by my personal views as they are expressed here.

This book should be approached as my own subjective synthesis and weighed evaluation of everything that I have ever read about Borderline Personality Disorder. Its goal is compassionate understanding and should not be used as a substitute for, alternative to, or practical adjunct in dealing with someone with BPD. It is a lay person's guide meant to stimulate greater interest in more authoritative sources by casting them in the oblique light of my own views. If this book brings out further dimensions or stimulates others to reconsider or revise their theoretical views of BPD in any way it has served its limited purpose.

As a further qualification, it would be presumptuous to suggest that I am in any way unique in applying contract terminology to BPD. My limited contribution here is my hope that the tendency to all-or-nothing solutions that is so common among people with this illness may be opposed by asking people with BPD over time to negotiate for what they want rather than demanding it and in doing so to recognize that they are not unique in the burdens that life imposes upon us. Persons with BPD often assume a sort of manipulative or adhesive quality, one that is alternately child-like and dictatorial, upon others. This attitude seems to proceed from the belief that they cannot manufacture from within themselves the confidence and capabilities that adult life demands.

When I use the term "contract" in this book I do so only analogically by drawing a parallel between legal contracts and our general negotiation process with the world. From the days of Rousseau's use of the term "Social Contract" to the days of modern contract theory represented by Corbin, Williston, and Rawls it has been fashionable to construe our adaptation to the necessities of life and to the demands of other people by drawing from contractual imagery. In this book I am suggesting that what is involved in the pathological processes of BPD may be clarified by appealing to the various ways that we negotiate with reality in order to survive and to achieve our goals.

The common mindset of many people with BPD is one that refuses or is unable to adequately engage with the shifting panorama of life that demands that concessions be made in order to achieve some measure of satisfaction of our needs and desires and to structure what might be called legitimate expectations from the self and others. One of the primary functions of law is to provide various processes to structure the world and to resolve conflicts by an appeal to an objective and verifiable set of standards that when all else fails can support consent and provide remedies. To remedy borderline characteristics is in many ways to rejoin the vernacular of human experience as manifested in legal theory.

This is not to say that Borderline patients are without dignity or that their perceptions are always inaccurate. I imply no direct moral judgments here. Instead, I believe that the composite character of BPD symptoms manifests an erroneous concept of the way that the world works and the seeming refusal to learn from experience among persons with BPD is due to the tendency to unilaterally impose their will upon persons and events because they perceive that any compromise will entail defeat. Defeat in turn is experienced by borderline patients as synonymous with overwhelming shame and even with a threat to their existence. I propose as a remedy the adoption of a model of definition and negotiation of terms so as to teach the skills of selective adaptation to consensual reality and to create in doing so a stable and realistic sense of self instead of the alternating states of helpless supplication and impulsive superiority that so often appear in those who suffer with BPD.

I also believe that Borderline Personality Disorder is a system rather than merely a person. BPD arises out of the patient's particular and unique history acting in conjunction with genetics and individual susceptibility. For this reason it is important to identify the subtle re-enforcers of Borderline pathology. These must be addressed if the identified patient is to improve. BPD represents the logical result of what might be called paradoxical reward systems that give the Borderline the message that she cannot regulate her own emotions, actions, or goals without filtering her experience through others. This causes persons with BPD to assume that they are alternatively and uniquely: powerful/helpless, entitled/unworthy, abandoning/abandoned, beautiful/ugly, and any of the other extreme dichotomies that life presents to us. As a result over time a storm is created within them much in the same way that a tropical pressure differential leads to the formation of a hurricane. Unlike the weather however that no one can control persons with BPD can over time begin to diffuse their own frenzied search for outside sources of order and support by:

1. Not feeding the storm by mindless compliance to their inner demands;

2. Gradually weaning themselves from paradoxical reward systems that only increase their feelings of resentment,

of inferiority, and deepen existing divisions within them by splitting;

3. These goals of personal containment may be aided by presenting and explaining how the urgent borderline demands, ones that are often based upon a sense of panic or identity diffusion, can be replaced by an increased ability to tolerate stress, delay gratification, test feelings over time for accuracy, and to re-evaluate their past coping strategies by learning new life skills;

4. Core changes occur from the outside in by breaking cycles of abuse and substituting healthy environmental cues and reflection for short-term impulsive coping mechanisms.

By taking a circumstantial and individual approach to all of the life-events that we must negotiate, persons with BPD may learn to resist the temptation to make vast generalizations based on feelings alone. This will help them to resist splitting rather than seeking to frame their experiences in consensual reality. With these changes a consistent and self-subsistent identity may be gradually formed within them over time.

Much of the crisis modality that has hitherto characterized their lives will pass and a healthy dynamism will supplant their former frantic efforts to control persons and events through jealousy, threats, verbal abusiveness, or isolation from others and from the human community. Contract formation may help to achieve these goals.

Introduction

There is a mystery involved in the very concept of what are called the Axis II Personality Disorders in the DSM. Even the concept of personality is largely dependent upon how we conceive what is most unique about a person and whatever theory we may favor or espouse regarding human development over the life course. It is difficult not to sound unduly judgmental or complacent when we presume to define a syndrome or recognize a pattern of habitual responses in another person as pathological or dysfunctional while at the same time hoping that the therapeutic process will result in a greater sense of cohesiveness and integrity in people who often experience extreme emotional distress at various times and whose relationships are often broken or unsatisfactory. If personality is largely situation dependent and socially conditioned and sustained then it is improper to focus solely on the identified patient as "the problem."

Lawyers are uniquely positioned to understand that much of what we call reality is transaction based and that transactions involve negotiation rather than being subject to unilateral commands or dictates. Attorneys understand the need that each of us feels to have at least one other human being to act as an advocate for us and to explain our needs and wants in more neutral language than may be readily available to ourselves because we are often too close to our own anxieties, stresses, and needs to see things clearly. The practice of law soon teaches its servants that words can act as only imperfect vehicles to understanding, that every text has its inherent ambiguities, and that the practical order of things is forever gnawing away at our desires to legislate a perfect world.

Those who have been trained in the majestic discipline of jurisprudence soon discover that almost everything is problematic and by saying this I mean to imply that no proposition no matter how self-evident it may appear is immune from scrutiny and questioning. The very habit of systematic doubt that many people with BPD manifest has its correlative in what lawyers do every day.

To represent a party requires that the lawyer adopt for the duration of the representation the client's point of view and to advance the client's interests within the parameters of the law. Zealous advocacy means using the tools of systemic thought, rhetorical expression, and his knowledge of human nature to help a client achieve his or her goals without unduly or unfairly burdening others. This means that lawyers if they are living up to the fullness of their calling seek out points of unity and compromise between conflicting interests rather than always seeking a hands-down win. The social fabric is maintained by doing minimal damage to others while pursuing the client's legitimate goals. Lawyers as servants of the court are obligated to interests beyond mere private representation and in this lawyers take justifiable pride. Along with the other professions lawyers are uniquely positioned to advance the general welfare and the progress of civilization.

The best way to think of this book is to compare it to what in music is called a fantasia or perhaps variations on a theme. It is an extended meditation upon the conditions that follow from a diagnosis of Borderline Personality Disorder as filtered through a mindset derived from training in a different field, that of the law. Lawyers are trained to draw distinctions and to think by analogy. Although the rule of precedent is respected, lawyers are accustomed to a rule of vigorous advocacy that may seek out weak places in prior chains of reasoning and to urge that changes should be made. Even evidence is carefully parsed according to the degree of assent that it should compel. Conflict is natural for lawyers although compromise is not to be eschewed. Even success on the merits of a case still requires that a proper remedy be devised to measure harms and to seek some measure of restitution.

There is a basic therapeutic intention in the pursuit of what might be called practical justice. Ideal solutions are often elusive and today's victory may upset the possibility of future productive consensual relations. This means that lawyers do not as a rule possess minds that accept any position as final at least not unless it has been thoroughly tested and litigated. Skeptical or idealistic as the circumstances demand, lawyers adapt themselves quickly to adverse circumstances and renew the assault. This would seem a proper set of traits to possess when dealing with the intractable symptoms of BPD.

I wish to state at the outset that this book is not a book of legal advice nor is it the result of a lawyer's reflections in dealing with Borderline clients. Instead it is an effort to apply the habits of mind that lawyers develop in the course of their training to what is often considered one of the most difficult and mysterious of mental disorders. Lawyers must often learn to see things from their client's point of view and in doing so develop their empathetic and listening skills. The task of advocacy is then to find a way to order the facts into a pattern to which the law may be applied to obtain a result that is in the client's best interest. At the same time lawyers are also officers of the court and counselors at law and as such must seek to harmonize individual self-interests of their clients with the demands of justice to other parties and to the laws of the commonwealth.

A properly functioning social order is one where individual needs are met in a reasonable manner while not overwhelming the social order through placing inordinate demands on resource allocation and distribution. It is because the demands of BPD can be so extreme that a lawyer's way of looking at things may be a valuable contribution to the therapeutic enterprise of mental health professionals. The dilemma of the person with Borderline Personality Disorder is in a way the problem of the entire human condition but written in italics and with capital letters and maybe one or two exclamation points as well.

Just as Sigmund Freud was able to generalize from problems of psychopathology to social history it is possible to read in the opposite direction and go from the general to the specific with BPD. History is nothing if it is not the record of the triumph of short-term interests, mistrust, and biased and partial perspectives over the interests of human progress and the common good of humanity. Similarly persons with BPD appear to be victims of an intrinsic willfulness that alternates with apparent helplessness in their futile efforts to control their emotions and actions. The results of this habit of mind can leave a record of a personal history that is lacking in the perfect standards that persons with BPD assume to be essential for a human being to attain if he or she is to be worthy to exist at all.

The disconnect between their impossibly high standards combined with a disrupted and discontinuous sense of self in their actual life history produces a sense of mourning for what has not actually been lost (because of never having really existed except in the realm of desire and of aspiration) but only seems to have been lost. A brief review of history will reveal waste on a scale that must make any individual feel some sense of confidence that in comparison their own lives have not been as bad as they may imagine. To correct course without condemnation or revenge is the task of maturity in both individuals and that of entire civilizations. This is not to diminish the tragedy of wasted opportunities in the life of the Borderline individual but to state clearly that real atonement is always positive and outer-oriented rather than being achieved by bitter remorse and self-hatred.

The title of this book implies that it is possible to cross borderlines much in the way that it is possible to navigate the check-points that exist at border patrol stations. This alone should convey a message of hope to persons who suffer from the mysterious condition that is called Borderline Personality Disorder. It is natural for a lawyer to question categories and definitions because the practice of law demands the use of this particular skill among many other skills and perspectives. Lawyers experience all categorizations as inherently problematic and subject to question in the service of clarification.

Just as the law is never a finished project so is the developmental course of an individual life never complete. For this reason to call someone a Borderline has often carried with it a reduction of the person to the dysfunctions that are often encountered in the course of their life-experience, but these dysfunctions by no means sum up the dignity and worth of the individual who exhibits them. It is the task of psychotherapy to help the person who suffers from BPD to increase their ability to navigate the predictable crises of life that can trigger the borderline patient's inadequate coping strategies. By having alternative response modes in place to diffuse anxiety, depression, or the focal self-damaging actions in which they often engage a new way of life can be slowly learned and internalized. By applying a wait and see attitude to the quick survival responses that can wreak havoc in relationships borderlines can slow the pace of response and avoid the panic followed by contrition cycles to which they are so often prone. Gradually it becomes possible to mourn the past and to let it go.

What Borderline individuals tend to believe, that they are radical exceptions to the usual course of human life, can gradually yield place to self-forgiveness and solidarity with the troubled human condition. The containment of reasonable expectations can yield a commitment to wellness rather than to an unreasonable search for perfection in their own lives or in that of others.

Trying to decide if there is an entity called Borderline Personality Disorder may therefore be less important than dealing with the constellation of disturbing inner images and actions that coalesce around the person who may be diagnosed with BPD. This is the approach that I will take in this book. It is natural for me to do so because as an attorney I can speak as an outsider and from that refracted point of view perhaps suggest an avenue of approach that may bring out certain features of BPD that are often missed by professional therapists, just as oblique lighting may bring out certain features in a painting. I will also be using the technique of motive analysis that attorneys use in the courtroom to try and analyze the built-in reward systems that may exist in any situation.

Lawyers learn to identify stakeholders and to seek points of agreement and reconciliation so as to maximize social good. From this perspective litigation should always be the last resort, at least in the case of private law. A much better model is that of contract which depends upon what lawyers call "bargained-for-exchange." Contracts are consensual agreements that benefit the parties to the contract.

What I will refer to as the Borderline Situation is characterized by enormous mental pain in the person with BPD combined with various concentric rings that are broadcast like transmissions from a radio tower to outlying destinations. The closer that one is to a person who exhibits borderline symptoms the more likely one is to witness and to be affected by what is going on within the depths of the personality of the person with BPD. The stress, pain, confusion, and friction that this can generate are disadvantageous for all involved. Rather than blame the borderline patient, who in any case probably spends a significant part of her life blaming herself, it seems to this writer to be more productive to analyze the structure of the situations in which the person with BPD may find himself or herself. Once typical situations can be defined it should be possible in theory at least to point out various coping strategies that may be better than the ones that immediately suggest themselves in the midst of their stress or panic.

I will leave it to various health professionals to suggest the therapy or causation questions that are more within their competence and training. As a lawyer I am less concerned with these questions than with actual human experience and the adequacy of verbal efforts to contain that experience. This will mean that this book will be systemic and phenomenological in its approach to BPD.

Phenomenology seeks to see without the distortion of applying preexisting ideas or formulations proceeding instead to an intuition of what the thing is in itself. As applied to BPD this will mean discussing how it feels to be a person with BPD. But this book will go further still and attempt to follow a systems theory that explains how the underlying entity (whatever that is in the case of BPD) generates the multiplicity of symptoms and contrasting characteristics that the borderline person may exhibit over time.

The theory that I will propose is that Borderline Systems of Behavior represent coded responses to stress that are caught up in various reverberations much like the screeching sound in a microphone feedback. The result of these coded responses is to evoke in others the shame and confusion that exists in the person with BPD. The result of this projective process over time for the person with BPD is isolation, broken relationships, and various types of self-harm that are used to diffuse and anaesthetize overwhelming pain by providing a focus for anger, guilt, resentment, or depression. BPD follows both an episodic and cyclic course, with periods of relative adaptation followed by relapses under stress or perceived abandonment or betrayal, which only confirms the alternations between states manifesting overweening pride followed by periods of complete self-doubt that many people with BPD experience.

The search for confirmation of their preexisting doubts consumes much of the lives of persons with BPD. Episodes of failure or betrayal are replayed in endless sequences, always looking for "the underlying truth." This habit of mind presumes that blame is easily fixed and always deserving of punishment and when the person with BPD is not punishing himself or herself, he or she is engaged in exacting either strict liability from someone else for perceived offenses or achieving a fixed and arbitrary stability by having identified the villain at last. Cycles of retribution follow each other with only one common denominator – the person with BPD feels that everything is aligned against him or her. Control and fixity become the goal of life. Surprises are lovely but the overriding suspicion always seems to put a worm in the apple of delight. Every instance of evidence of good faith and good will on the part of others becomes just one more disguise for a betrayal that will be all the more catastrophic for its long delay when it finally comes.

For this reason persons with BPD would rather drive others away quickly while they can still harbor some hope that they are good and not yet infected with the general badness that they feel all about them, and worse, existing within themselves. The fact that badness is not a disembodied ghost haunting the world but simply a judgment of partial situations does not occur to the person with BPD because the overriding world view is one of alternating absolutes. A thing or person is either all good or all bad. This explains the haunted quality of BPD perceptions. Fluffy poodles may be transformed into ravenous grizzly bears at a moment's notice. Worse still, the person with BPD may suddenly experience herself as morphing into what she most despises and judges within herself. There is no effective model of forgiveness to help her to negotiate these crises of self-worth which she experiences viscerally in every fiber of her being.

Sensitivity to slights that may start the avalanche of self-blame keeps the Borderline Person perpetually on guard. This results in the cyclic rhythm of agony that makes Borderline Personality Disorder so distressing to experience or to witness by loved ones or friends. But the hopelessness that results need not lead to more acting out. Instead, a remedial approach may adopt an alternative to the all or nothing bathwater temperature of the borderline's world where she is either scalding or freezing.

It is time for a remedy and I believe that contract principles applied analogically may provide one. These on-going contracts negotiated with significant others can act as a mode of identifying common themes in each Borderline Person's individual constellation of experience of the world and relationships. This constellation of symptoms may be augmented with new structures to provide nurturance and support and to set up coping strategies before the crises materialize and help the person with BPD to deal with life's inevitable ups and downs. People without BPD do this unconsciously and habitually while with BPD making these contracts is an acquirable skill. This book will explain how this may be done.

The approach to BPD explored in this volume is a practical one and not a substitute for psychiatric or psychological intervention. Instead, this book advocates what might be described as individualized life-course training combined with a reflection on general values. While not acting as a lawyer or discussing ways that attorneys may encounter Borderlines in their professional practice, this book uses a general jurisprudential and reflective habit of mind that is natural to attorneys and by this means I attempt a phenomenology of Borderline Personality Disorder. My proposed audience is anyone who must deal with the Borderline Situation in their lives or anyone who has felt the influence or gravitational pull that is exerted like a force field by someone who manifests BPD in their lives.

As therapies have evolved understanding has filled in many of the gaps of our knowledge about BPD and of ways of coping with it. Borderline Personality Disorder was at one time a holding category for difficult patients that appeared to bridge the gap between neurosis and psychosis. BPD is now part of a cluster of what are termed disorders in personality development and subsequent behaviors. It is impossible to escape all pejorative connotations associated with such a diagnosis. In addition many Borderlines manifest co-occurring and overlapping personality disorders or a spectrum of dysfunctions that makes it questionable whether the parameters of BPD are ever strictly definable diagnostically. For this reason the most salutary therapies to date emphasize a pragmatic approach that is adaptable to the actual and unique needs of each BPD patient.

Psychotherapy with a person with BPD will always manifest a certain triage component for the simple reason that Borderlines do not surrender control willingly for extended periods of time. The goal of therapy is to leave some residue of better coping skills and some degree of self-insight into their inner ego states in patients with BPD. The rest of the cure is often merely a function of time. Life appears to be its own best tutor where human beings are concerned. The task for the Borderline is to negotiate life as we all must with all of its contingencies and uncertainties. It is here that the acute sensitivity of the Borderline meets the intractable demands of living. If friction between the two can be reduced by lowering demands as negotiation and compromise demand then life will consequently be easier for the person with BPD.

Contracts manifest less than ideal agreements that enhance situational values through compromise and concession. To approach life then under the parameter of a negotiation process is already to make it possible to imagine a better and less painful way to live. It is my hope that this book may prove to be a useful contribution to those ends of peace, mindfulness, and integration so that the diagnosis of BPD may over time be replaced by the relative health that we presume to term normality and that the seeds of jealousy and discontent that often afflict those with BPD who seek in love the answer to all their ills may be quieted in a general affection for friends and a wider sphere of support and community in their daily lives.

The first question in dealing with what are today called Axis Two Disorders in the various updated editions of the Diagnostic and Statistical Manual used by mental health workers since the DSM-III was published in 1980 to include the Borderline Personality Disorder diagnostic criteria is whether BPD is primarily an example of an underlying biological predisposition or is the result of sexual abuse or other traumas that may produce this devastating and ineffective life-strategy.

The type of treatment chosen to treat BPD will depend upon where along this spectrum from determinism to free-will BPD patients are located. If a strict disease model is chosen through which to view the chaotic behaviors of someone with BPD then the person with BPD is evaluated as existing at a level of primitive psychological defenses and the therapy must of necessity be more globally supportive. As the person with BPD functions at higher levels and demonstrates that she may employ higher level psychological defenses various expressive therapies that depend upon insight and control may supplant the containment provided by exterior structures such as in-patient care.

Contemporary therapy approaches hold out the hope that new life-skills can be taught and new and more adaptive strategies can be substituted for the old patterns of response that are characteristic of BPD. At the same time, biological factors may be addressed with anti-depressants or other psychotropic medications to aid the psychotherapy. The most commonly used psychotherapeutic tools today in dealing with BPD are the Cognitive-Behavioral Therapy devised by Marsha Linehan and the various Psycho-Dynamic expressive therapies that proceed by helping the borderline patient to gain insight into the patterns of BPD while learning to diminish various acting-out behaviors and to substitute verbal communication and behavioral controls for impulsive and often self-destructive actions.

As progress is made to contain affects and to grow in patience over time many of the elements that confirm a BPD diagnosis may begin to diminish until they are no longer applicable. At this point the BPD entity becomes less of an actual present condition and retains instead only an underlying tendency that can be specially monitored at times of particular stress so as to ease the passage through the various crises that are entailed in living in an uncertain world.

Unfortunately patients with BPD often leave therapy prematurely because the same defense of splitting that they use in other areas of their lives is applied to the therapist. The motives and competence of the therapist are questioned and devalued and the Borderline simply walks away with her dominant oscillating world-views intact. Desperate for help persons with BPD all too often push it away with both hands when it is actually offered to them. BPD may be approached philosophically then as a disorder that implicates both the perceptual faculties and the will as well. Persons with a BPD personality configuration demonstrate that they experience the world in swiftly changing and variable contours. This results in an inner sense of desperation that causes them to act out in impulsive and dramatic gestures in order to manifest their inner pain to others and to get what they want through unilateral actions that may be traced back to their perceptual fragmentation.

I would like to comment here on the often reported sense of emptiness and boredom that persons with BPD often report experiencing. At first glance this may seem to contrast with the exquisite sensitivity that is also experienced by people with BPD and the energy that may be manifest at the times in their impulsive or angry reactions. Their emptiness and boredom are the predictable results of the imbalance in their lives.

The lack of correspondence between their affects and actions create painful life results for them. True vitality proceeds from intelligent and reflectively directed force rather than from mere febrile reactivity.

The contributions of several phenomenological philosophers are relevant here. The French philosopher, Henri Bergson, and later the phenomenological psychologist, Eugene Minkowski, wrote extensively about what they called the Élan Vital. There exists within us a force that impels us into the future. This force may be affected by various moods and affects but fundamentally it is a sense that time is a negotiable modality of experience. Lived time is not the same as chronological time. Lived time instead is time as experienced by the Élan Vital as it projects itself into the future.

The emptiness and boredom reported by borderline patients could be spoken of in phenomenological terms as an inhibition of the life project such that the future appears either as an abyss or as one lacking all landmarks of personal significance such that the future ceases to be personalized. Time becomes mere succession rather

than what it must be for the Élan Vital to be actualized. Human beings are defined by the ability to plan and to anticipate results. It is the legacy of the eternal still existing within us. BPD can on occasion cause a dislocation in this perception of the self as projected into the future so that the patient becomes de-personalized and experiences the body as a mere object in space as opposed to being the basis of a dynamic trajectory into the fully lived present. The life project becomes stalled and depression is its manifest symptom.

Vitality feeds on communication with the self and with others. The isolation that is experienced by Borderline patients tends to leave them stalled by the side of the highway of life with no particular or achievable goal or destination in mind. It is at this point that the person with BPD naturally seeks some means to restore vitality. Love is often the chosen path. The Borderline patient seeks to replace a personal Élan Vital with a symbiotic relationship with another. As the self/object boundaries dissolve the Borderline feels a desperate need to preserve this idealized relation at all costs while simultaneously recognizing the impossibility of a perfect merger with another person without compromising his or her own fragile sense of individuality. The sheer totality of the aspirations to such a controlled relationship condemns it to failure.

Much of the conflict in borderline relationships is caused by the disappointment entailed by a failure to individuate and to separate while still retaining a relationship with the world and with other people. This vacillation in approach/avoidance behaviors is what is called "splitting" in various discussions of Borderline Personality Disorder. The abrupt valence changes from positive to negative and back again are nothing less than a survival response that makes manifest the intense ambivalence of the borderline person's feelings about herself and the world. The impulsivity and acting-out behaviors are similarly motivated by a desire to rely upon change or stimulation, by pain or danger, in order to restore the vital flow of life and to dispel the sense of deadness, pointlessness, emptiness, or of being stalled or stuck that is so present and painful within them.

These feelings of oppression are a logical result of a loss of a sense of vitality and what Eugene Minkowski calls lived time. When the sense of vitality does not flow readily from within them persons with BPD tend to look elsewhere for solace by finding in another person a desperately chosen adjunct to their own being. Other people and particularly therapists or other attachment figures are presumed to be able to infuse life into the person with BPD such that their dreadful feelings of shame, fear, anxiety, or desolation will go away.

People with Borderline Personality Disorder often cannot conceive of love except as bondage and control. In the struggle for mastery they often kill that which they would wish to preserve by compulsively grasping what can only be freely offered. This only adds to their sense of alienation and isolation. It takes wisdom to counter false ideas and openness to the future to offer an anodyne to past regrets. Borderline individuals often experience things in powerful impressions and intuitive leaps rather than in causal chains and evidence-based generalizations.

For this reason past experiences are of only marginal use to them. Only what is present and immediate exists for them. Though their intellectual and reality-testing abilities are not usually impaired, symbolic communication may be preferable in dealing with them rather than arguing or explanation. An immediate and intuitive appeal is of greater force to convince them than all that a more left-brain approach would counsel. This realization is of importance to therapists who hope to help persons with BPD to make progress. To understand what the person with BPD is feeling is a thousand times more effective than merely pointing out where their true interests lie since the Borderline does not exist in a stable world of well-considered choices but in a world of insistent and contradictory demands upon which the Borderline feels her very existence depends.

To seek the unqualified good of the client or patient as doctors and attorneys are trained to do is often to stand alone since borderline patients are often bonded over time to pain and to habits of self-abuse. The better thing is to ride out the present storm and do what good one can when opportunity offers to shore up their ego defenses and to show them a path through the minefield of their own dark conceptions. One step forward and two steps back is often the order of the day.

The final goal of therapy is to help the person with BPD to negotiate the developmental hurdle of separation/individuation while still retaining the ability to stay in relation without either being engulfed or abandoned. The balance and acceptance of a universe where ambivalence, change, and conflict can be negotiated rather than avoided is as good a definition of a cure for BPD as I can recommend. The demands of reality testing take the place of the former determination of the person with BPD to prevail at all costs over recalcitrant circumstances. Humility and forgiveness become more habitual rather than presuming that anything less than perfection will cause love to die and send her hurdling outward like a planet unleashed from the sun into dark and endless space.

Helping professionals of all sorts often like things to be settled and completed but dealing with the issues posed by the Borderline Personality Disorder is often as impossible as controlling the weather. There is even debate as to whether therapy is the best approach in dealing with persons whose primitive level defenses may be seen as essential to whatever ego integrity they may still possess. No therapeutic effort is without risk and no approach to another person can hope for more than to relieve needless pain to some degree and to empower the patient to seek a deeper and more fulfilling life. After doing this one should surrender the illusion of control and try to learn over time how to dance in the rain.

Thomas Mengert, J.D.

Chapter One

Overview of BPD

The title of this book speaks of negotiating not with the Borderline person but rather with the Borderline Personality as though the personality constellation is in some way severable from the totality of the person. I would like to say at the outset that this is more a gesture of hope than of certainty that such a negotiation can ever take place. To those therapists who deal daily with individuals with BPD this title may sound as though it was written in the same sanguine spirit as that shown by the English when seeking peace with Fascist Germany over the issue of the fate of the Sudetenland.

The general approach to life of persons with BPD is often similarly dictatorial and unyielding, refusing all concessions. Pain inflicted and received becomes over time a milieu that is no longer resisted because pain seems to define their very sense of self. Borderlines tend to push away all efforts to empathize with their pain or to point out alternatives that would ease their passage through life.

For this reason many mental health professionals are reluctant to treat them. Not only is the therapy likely to be a lengthy one, it will in addition entail various efforts by the patient to disrupt the therapy and to test the personal resources of the therapist or the in-house staff of mental health facilities. The anger that these patients may provoke may raise doubts about the reasons why resources should be allocated to individuals who seem so selfish and obnoxious by ordinary standards of behavior.

Why try and save people who may often display various addictions, promiscuity, mercurial moods, and temper tantrums? Why try and save people who in every way possible seem to be saying, "Just leave me alone and let me go to hell in my own way!" After awhile the mere word, "Borderline" can cause an involuntary clenching of teeth and protective gestures to guard vulnerable or soft areas of one's own personality and to protect the therapist's sense of professional competence and sense of self-worth.

The literature on BPD is divided between books that try and elicit compassion and aid for people with this diagnosis and other books explaining how to cope with or to recover from encounters with them. The symptoms of BPD are pervasive in the daily functioning of individuals who are at the same time often overwhelmingly brutal towards the feelings of others while remaining fragile and vulnerable in themselves. Extremes are courted daily while the middle-ground remains virtually unoccupied. Caught between the polar extremes of their behavior most people can only wince, duck, and cover. References to their characteristic splitting of affect will tend to recur in any book about BPD.

It is impossible to remain value-neutral to such a harmful set of behaviors and dispositions. It is for this reason that I speak of negotiating with the disease and not the person. Antagonism should be re-directed from the person to the syndrome which can then be opposed in its relentless course of destruction. The effort to pry someone loose from the grasp of BPD is at times like attempting surgery on an inoperable cancer. When the metastasis-like tendrils of BPD have so co-opted the energy of the personality recovery must proceed from within rather than from any outside intervention no matter how well meant such efforts may be.

If this book's sole purpose however to counsel despair however it need not have been written. If no negotiation with that entity called BPD was possible then all cases would simply be dismissed as terminal. This dark vision does not square with what is known of BPD. Certain types of therapy can indeed offer support to those patients who are willing to reach out and grasp the life-preserver or safety-ring that is waving about in front of them on the stormy seas of their lives. The very fragility of their ego-structures though tends to make Borderlines reluctant to admit mistakes in their coping skills or to trust others when they may have already pre-determined that everyone will eventually abandon them. Borderline individuals are past-masters at the skill of the self-fulfilling prophesy. They serve as the writer, the producer, and the director of various sordid and distressing dramas that fill their desolate days and lonely nights. Life proceeds around them lovely and undiminished while their shadowy forms haunt various jails, mental wards, or the streets. Others find support and sustenance in the penumbra of other people's forbearance and endurance and at times suspend the chaos and distress of their lives for a time.

Such is the life of a person with BPD to one degree or another. If the illness is justly to be abjured however this does not mean that this condemnation should be extended to its chief victims. A person is not synonymous with a disease process no matter how far its maleficent course has advanced. There is always hope for the person. Make no mistake though: BPD is not a viable condition; it must be opposed and its advances thwarted. This book is an effort in that direction.

A book such as this is necessarily brief because it is meant to serve as a footnote to what has already been said about Borderline Personality Disorder by those better qualified to explain and treat it. What is new in my approach is derived from the fact that an attorney is writing it, which is to say approaching it from the unique perspective that legal training bestows upon the human mind. It is being written in tandem with a book on reforming the legal system and it is anyone's guess which topic presents greater challenges.

Persons with Borderline Personality Disorder or BPD are considered by psychotherapists as I have already mentioned above to be some of their most difficult and exasperating patients. Borderline persons are reputed to be demanding, manipulative, irascible, subject to swift contradictions, and to acting out their feelings rather than restraining them and exploring alternatives before acting. All of this is contrary to the mindset of the legal mind. Lawyers are trained to verbalize everything and to never consent to anything unless every possible consequence is sounded out and provided for. If Borderlines are reckless, lawyers are cautious; if Borderlines act without thinking, lawyers often think without acting. Lawyers seek to find optimal solutions while Borderlines seek instinctually to polarize and to divide. Borderlines presume ill-intent and opposition and thus usually provoke rejection to confirm their doubts and fears. Lawyers seek to elaborate general policies and rules to guide future conduct by precedent whereas Borderlines approach every situation de novo and seem as a result never to learn from past experience. The result is that the lives of people with BPD often resemble one of those chain-reaction accidents on the interstate highways with vehicles strewn about and tire-tracks everywhere. The question is always where to begin to set the situation right.

It has seemed to me that the best way is to seek to understand the world of the Borderline as it is experienced for experienced it really is; Borderline Persons are not simulating their distress. If Borderlines manifest confusion it may be because they are in fact often overwhelmed by thoughts, feelings, and impulses that will not be contained. Their emotiveness is real and not simulated for effect. This book will attempt to provide the same overview of BPD that a helicopter news-crew might obtain over a crash-scene from a point of view that will allow the shape and contours of BPD to emerge.

The concept of a personality disorder implies that a more functional and normative life alternative exists and that proper maturation and ego integrity will usually be such that no diagnostically defined "disorder" will be said to be present. Particularly in the case of Borderline Personality Disorder it is impossible to ignore the presumptions and normative values that are in a sense smuggled in along with the diagnosis. Persons with BPD combine emotional reactivity with finely-tuned perceptions that will pick up on any degree of withdrawal or alienation in other people. If persons with BPD fear abandonment it is just possible that they have often been betrayed or abandoned. If they are suspicious it may be that they have often been victims of excessive trust. If they are abrasive and demanding it may be because they exist along the knife-edge cliff of their personal dissolution and despair. The drama that they are living out may have been written in a distant land by a remote ancestor the legacy of whose life is passed along as familial shame, guilt, or various secrets. In their most vulnerable years many persons with BPD have been passive recipients of the projected fear or depression of their surroundings. There is a base-tone of existence that can blight entire historical eras and sub-groups of populations that can embody what can only be termed generational disease. Often these feelings are anchored in various religious strictures or interpretations. As these words are being written a case appeared in the news of the beating death of one teenage boy and the serious condition of his brother. They were beaten by their mother, father, and sister on Church premises to get them to confess their sins for the good of their souls. America is a nation that is renowned for its gun violence, mass-killings in schools, and proxy wars fought in various foreign lands. It is probable that many aspects of BPD are not strictly personal in origin but rather a response to social factors in the environment.

Does BPD so often appear in young females because of the innate conflicts faced by young women in a society that gives them conflicting role expectations and holds them to demanding external standards for identity and self-worth? Is BPD an example of social battle-fatigue as certain sensitive souls attempt to adapt to expectations that cannot nurture or embrace their uniqueness and particular gifts? Is the defensive stance that they so often adopt a rational response to the life circumstances from which they have come? These and similar questions must be born in mind in all that follows to bracket any generalizations or assumptions that somewhere there exists a standard from whence deviations can be plotted on the graph of a "normal" personality. Persons with BPD though in pain and often beset by loneliness are unfortunately often seen as beyond the pale and consigned to that outer region where we exile those who remind us too clearly of our own discomforts and our primal insecurities

The primal experience of the Borderline individual is that of abandonment and exile. The various assertive personae that cycle through the lives of Borderlines as successive coping vehicles are false selves rather than evidence of real self-possession. To possess a true self is to be mirrored and affirmed without being used or absorbed by another person. Love requires mutuality without diminution. No human being can be a mere appendage of or to another human being. We must each of us bear the burden of maintaining a separate existence without succumbing to terror or despair as we seek relatedness to the world that we share with other persons. The task that Borderline Persons face is that of the search for individuation.

Many Borderlines in relationships reach the false conclusion that only by maintaining perfect control of other people can love be maintained. Borderlines alternate between attitudes of desire and repulsion towards their own bodies, their lovers, and the world. The normal rhythms of life are reduced to a series of frantic and ultimately self-defeating acts of the will as the Borderline tries to force maturation without the proper tools. Those tools can only be acquired by trust maintained towards a stable and reliable source of unconditional affirmation that brings to birth the stable sense of self that eludes them in life and makes dealing with others so problematic and painful for them. Negotiating to produce a stable environment and source of figures that can provide a stable template for the self is what psychotherapy seeks to achieve.

People with BPD exist in a state of chaos analogous to a nuclear reactor that is constantly at a risk of meltdown. The two reasons for this are first of all an exquisite sensitivity to vastly conflicting emotional states and second a lack of a cohesive concept of self to provide a containment vehicle for daily living in the world. Lacking a sense of interior stability Borderlines use other people and manipulate situations so as to retain an illusion of control of their world. The defense that has been called "splitting" is a method of creating strict barriers between the good-self/bad-self and the good-other/bad-other. Grandiosity and helplessness alternate in a Borderline's life.

To observe a Borderline in a state of meltdown is to watch a person alternating swiftly between ego-states much like watching a television cycling through channels. The effect is often uncannily like watching a person in the grip of possession and it is possible that Borderlines manifest a degree of pain and dysfunction analogous but still not identical to what invasion by an outer evil entity would manifest. At the central core of BPD there exists an archaic and undeveloped central personality that functions like the eye at the center of a hurricane. When this central self manifests it is calm and even wise and profoundly lovable.

It is this core persona that calls out for help and often draws unwary mariners onto the rocks of relationships with the Borderline person when the storm winds rise again. To allow the Borderline to in a sense call the shots is to live in the Borderline's own desolate and stormy world. This is what is meant by the defense that is called "projective identification," which is experienced as a sense of shame and helplessness as the Borderline probes for weaknesses, character flaws, or points of vulnerability in other people to justify their own lack of trust in human relationships and sense of past betrayal at the hands of others. There is always a list of former friends or loved ones who have since been categorized as enemies. No amount of prior good service or fidelity will entitle a therapist, lover, or friend to any residual good-will and confidence once the tide has changed. The final balance account always reads zero. Borderlines live in a constant state of allocating blame between their own actions and those of others – depressed one moment and contrite they will shift with lightening-like speed to engage in a third-degree interrogation and accusation of those whom they claim to love. A wounded sparrow at one moment, they will be transformed in an instant into a roaring lion seeking someone to devour.

To inhabit a world in close proximity to a Borderline is to run the same risk of exposure that besets the Borderline on a daily basis. Those who are not able to bear the strain, the abuse, and the fear for the Borderline's own safety may either leave, break down themselves, or become so stilted and rehearsed in their responses that they cease to relate to the Borderline in a sustained and human way and are discarded as the hollow people that they have become like dry skeletal remains of flies caught in a spider's web. Borderlines are no more merciful to themselves than the spider is to the fly – she is both victim and victimizer. This is the central contradiction of BPD and part of what makes it so puzzling, frustrating, and ultimately self-defeating.

Much has been written about the concept of "containment" where Borderline individuals are concerned. Borderlines suffer from identity diffusion, out of control emotions, and even periodic dissociation into psychotic states. Their lives are often spent in damage control when periods of comparative calm follow periods of acting-out with various addictions or projections of their pain and confusion upon others. The proposed contract model that I am proposing here is designed to give the Borderline a sense of containment and security by framing their behavior issues and specifying consequences. Contracts are binding not through oppression or imposition but rather as the fruit of compromise and active freedom. Rather than being prisoners of their own whims and reversals Borderlines can look forward to the contract as a "containment vehicle" and a source of security. At the same time people who relate to the Borderline Situation will be given a chance to understand the very special demands imposed upon Borderline individuals by virtue of their condition of laboring under the demands of their illness.

Specificity and mapping are the keys. It is imperative to understand as a starting point then what it is like to live in the world of a person with BPD. The swift reversals, the contradictions, the impulsive actions, the paradoxical efforts to find inner solace through pain, the provocations and manipulations, all may assume a common meaning when specific instances are recorded and common elements are sought. By connecting cause and effect and reviewing the quick steps of her mental processes that often lead to faulty conclusions the person with

BPD can see new patterns and grow in self-understanding. She may then begin to imagine alternatives to the customary ways of dealing with her feelings. As new skills develop and better results are obtained the person with BPD may be willing to commit to further specific contractual commitments. The process of negotiation is renewed as progress is made and new remedies are devised as the situation demands. Imagination and persistence in a supportive milieu are the prerequisites of progress. While not all contingencies may be contracted for, the very process of negotiation creates habits of communication, consultation, and compromise. These habits are of the essence in forming what psychologists term a therapeutic alliance. This alliance must be supported by similar agreements concluded with other significant others in the patient's life.

What I am suggesting here is that the process of therapy may itself be overly focused by creating an artificial dyad forcing the therapist to function not only as an analyst but as a role model for the patient as they adopt and adapt to a new mode of life. Any re-parenting process runs into the same problem that often leads to BPD in the first place – a poor fit between parents and the BPD patient. Can a therapist really fill the role of being a template for a new personality structure while retaining the necessary objectivity to confront and explain how the present behaviors stemming from BPD are damaging the patient's life?

Much of what is called transference in psycho-therapy is caused by the fact that we ask too much of what is after all only a single if important relationship in the patient's life. When the commercial nature of the therapy transaction is factored in and the need for the therapist to retain a private life even while treating his patients it can be seen that many borderline patients feel that the skills learned in therapy originated in a hothouse environment where alone they can thrive; they cannot be depended upon in the cold cruel world. Even the most supportive therapy often cannot provide the safety zone that many people with BPD need when they are sent back into unhealthy environments. These environments themselves must be negotiated. How many hours are in a week? How few hours in therapy? How much wreckage of the past remains to be healed? This is the reason that therapy with Borderlines so often fails; it is simply not up to the stresses placed upon it.

Chapter Two

Excavating Deeper Dimensions

Part of the personal and interpersonal stress of BPD is caused by what might be called a flight of ideas. Like a rolling snowball growing in size with each moment the strong emotions of someone with BPD can grow with startling rapidity once certain circuits are triggered. People with BPD feel that they are always engaged on crossing bridges that may collapse underneath them without warning. This means that everything is treated as provisional and various perceptions or even convictions may be magically transformed into their opposite without warning.

Borderlines tend to prefer either chaos or isolation. The speed of their mental processes can sift data with remarkable speed and sometimes uncanny accuracy but then they may go on to experience times that are characterized by periods of lethargy, depression, and feelings of abandonment accompanied by a feeling of being terminally unique. In their relentless search for a self-definition people with BPD may vacillate between childlike naiveté and bitter mistrust and cynicism. Today's hero may become yesterday's villain overnight. This same tendency to instant revaluation is also applied to the Borderline herself; from exaltation she may be plunged into the depths of despair, shame, or disgust by a chance event or comment. What seems most difficult is to heal the chasm across ambivalence and to withhold premature judgments and actions that can swiftly cause minor incidents to spin out of control. My own review of the literature on BPD has made it clear to me that persons with BPD spend much of their life searching for what might be called, "perfect empathic mirroring." The intensity and variability of borderline emotional responses makes life difficult for them on a daily basis. The more unique their experiences appear to be and the greater that their mistrust and isolation becomes, the greater the deficit grows between what they need and what they have received.

Many people with BPD grow up with a profound mismatch between parent and child. Sometimes this is caused by being raised in a home-life environment that includes alcoholism in one or both parents, career instability, frequent changes of location or schools, or excessive expectations in the family dynamic for wealth, social success, or redemption of past failures. The child may feel that to fail is simply unacceptable and that a strict record is being kept of various occasions when results have come up short of what was expected of them. Experimentation and individuation require an ability to take risks and to make mistakes without forfeiting the respect and affection that she requires from significant others. Much of the frustration and excessive rage that people with BPD experience may be caused by the presence within them of what might be called "impacted resentments." Borderline persons keep a catalogue of the occasions when they have failed and when others have failed them. It may feel as if life has been one long period of trials and tests and that nothing has ended up the way that it was supposed to. This makes the disablement of the BPD condition even more difficult to bear because having a mental illness was simply not part of the program that the borderline may have projected for her life course. The mourning that this causes makes Borderlines feel stuck in a cycle of failed relationships, abandoned projects, and changing life-goals. The search for some sort of global key that will efface the past, secure the present, and open a vista to the future seems to elude them while yet being absolutely possible and to be expected. *"Why does it just work out for everybody else? What is their secret? What's wrong with me anyway?"*

As the gap between their projected life and their actual life grows wider, the emotional volatility of a person with BPD only increases; depression and self-blame alternate with a sense that she has been betrayed. Like an electric charge of static electricity she carries about with her, the Borderline has a tendency to painfully "zap" anyone who comes too near to her. This tends to drive other people away from her. Each failure only increases her sense of being different, flawed, or toxic. What she most desires and needs is precisely what she cannot find. Worse still this brings on bouts of intense psychological pain. The impulsive actions, substance abuse, and self-destructive acts which are characteristic of BPD are simply manifestations of her efforts to manage an increasingly chaotic set of life circumstances and conflicted inner feelings about herself, other people, and the world.

Perhaps the best single image of what it feels like to experience BPD is to use the phrase "emotional vertigo." Things and perceptions are always shifting about. Perceptions can alter without actually being hallucinations. Information content may be radically different from day to day or even from hour to hour; this phenomenon is often referred to in the literature on BPD as intense emotional liability. Borderlines tend to experience more intensely and more variably. Some mental health practitioners explain these characteristics by positing a dysfunction of the amygdala which regulates the fight or flight response and feelings of fear and anxiety. When people with BPD feel threatened ordinary interchanges or common disappointments may appear as disasters requiring an immediate and extreme defensive response or counter-attack. Much of Borderline impulsiveness is ultimately traceable to the overwhelming feelings that may be easily triggered by outer events or by one of the various habitual attribution structures that each Borderline person possesses. Templates of mistrust may exist based upon past traumas.

When chaotic feelings emerge it is natural to try and solve the problem by referring back to similar occasions when the same feelings were present. As a problem-solving skill this is a natural human response but in someone with BPD this review can serve to bring forth the former occasions in all of their initial distress. The past is preserved in the person with BPD with much of its emotional content still intact like a buried and unexploded bomb. Any present distress is likely to trigger an avalanche of recollections of similar instances. These enter the present moment until in short order the coping strategies normally provided by memory are overwhelmed. Everything is happening simultaneously. This naturally causes a sense of panic to set in. It is then that people with BPD seek out immediate solace to deal with the pain and to block the perceptual flood that they are experiencing.

One of the most common of these paradoxical sources of solace is to self-inflict focal pain. This process is sometimes referred to as "cutting." Rather than being simply an attention-getting behavior or dramatic gesture, cutting functions in the following way: By making the injury exterior rather than interior it becomes visible and seemingly more manageable. The wound is also symbolic and for this reason more meaningful than the vague distress of an inner feeling. Physical pain is also distracting because something must be done about it such as bandaging the wound or cleaning up the mess. This in turn gives the person with BPD a sense of power and control that helps her to combat the rising feeling of panic or distress. There is also a self-punitive component operative here because persons with BPD often blame themselves for their feelings as though feelings were deliberate and culpable decisions or acts. Finally, cutting produces pain which in turn triggers the release of endorphins in the brain and may cause a general calming effect.

When cutting is not the coping mechanism of choice then other self-destructive acts such as alcohol abuse, illegal drug-use, or reckless behaviors of all types may serve the same function. These coping mechanisms share in common a symbolic or paradoxical quality which serves to displace the anxiety or problem and to solve it by various magical gestures.

Because the world of the person with BPD is so fragile and unstable many people with BPD spend significant time and effort in environmental monitoring and control. The world is experienced as vaguely threatening or malicious or at other times as vastly empty and indifferent. More extroverted persons with BPD may seek to impose their will onto any situation or group by immediately taking control, often through splitting or using various dramatic gestures to polarize opposition. But these same people who appear so powerful and manipulative when shamed or in doubt can experience their inner nature as vastly unworthy and deserving of punishment.

More introverted people with BPD create the same sense of control of their environment through isolation and by maintaining strict control over access and egress of things or people in their lives. Inanimate objects may be invested with almost personal qualities. The need for order and for special bonding with these objects may appear to be examples of hoarding or symptomatic of Obsessive-Compulsive Disorder but in the person with BPD the function is more than just the relief of anxiety. Each object is an integral part of the exterior world and at the same time part of a web of inner associations that though invisible to others is real to the person with BPD, as real as if each object was mapped on an architectural drawing or placed in a still-life painting. There is a sacred and almost religious quality to this mode of perceiving the world that provides a source of inner solace.

The world of the person with BPD is a dialectical world caught between extremes. Chaotic acting-out may alternate with seeking refuge in comforting and safe places much in the way that someone might cross a raging stream by stepping from rock to rock and heaving a sigh of relief after reaching the other side. By maintaining a radical division of perceptions and valuations the borderline strategy seeks to avoid the unwelcome surprises that may trigger a descent into the vortex of pain.

I will conclude this discussion of what it feels like to have BPD by explaining that the pain that comes with these emotional storms can be intense and overwhelming. It is this fact that should awaken compassion for those who experience BPD. It is also a major reason why persons with BPD should seek out and pursue the effective therapies which are now available for their condition. The most significant task of these therapy processes is convincing the person with BPD that there is an alternate way to experience the world and to cope with life's inevitable challenges and shortcomings. Rather than seeking for a single universal answer or perfect solution, patients in recovery learn that concepts have fuzzy edges and that it is possible to exist in a middle-ground of ambiguity. It is safe to surrender power, to defer gratification, to withhold judgment, to defer punishment, to forgive, and to suspend conclusions; in other words it is possible to let life be what life is and to ride the waves rather than to be constantly struggling just to keep one's head above water.

By gradually acquiring new coping skills in a supportive and enlightened setting that honors and comprehends what the person with BPD has been going through, healing can occur. The underlying physiological basis of BPD may remain but the upsets now have a background based upon new beliefs and better coping skills. This lessens the pain and relieves the serial failures that are the result of many of the former symptomatic characteristics of BPD.

Sometimes time and merely growing older has served to heal people with BPD. Life is the great educator. Our demands are modulated when laid against the vast conflagrations of history. Private issues assume their proper context when laid against the vast panorama of human loss and triumph in adversity. Hope is rekindled when it is seen that the human spirit triumphs again and again against odds that seem insurmountable. When it is recalled that the single greatest tragedy of the human race was the rejection of love when offered in the person of Our Lord yet the resurrection followed, it can be affirmed in faith that human life is ultimately more than we can ever conceive. We surrender to grace and let God suffice as the ground of all our being and our final goal.

It is important to understand Borderline Personality Disorder because the disorder has a profound social dimension. Anyone who deals with a person with BPD is likely to recall the encounter just as people recall various natural phenomena like earthquakes and hurricanes. Persons with BPD are mysterious but not subtle. There is an energy aura about them that can verge on the uncanny. This very difference can awaken responses in other people that are primitive and primal. Perhaps people with BPD recall our own suppressed childhood fears and memories when we are in their company. Polarization seems to follow them like a shadow and they are as likely to be a victim as a victimizer. Blame and shame accompany their every action and provide a general ambiance of mistrust. Dread and fear pervade their decisions as though any action might elicit a train of irreparable misfortunes. All aspects of life tend to become tarnished as the disease progresses and hopes continually betrayed are endlessly replayed as though the past could somehow be given a gloss that would restore its promises. Alternating between ecstasy and despair Borderlines have trouble accepting life's inherent ambiguities and disappointments without yielding to anger or a sense that they are hopelessly flawed.

This would be bad enough, but persons with BPD are often beset by what are called co-morbid states such as depression, Obsessive Compulsive Disorder, substance-abuse issues, and various identity disturbances. BPD existed for many years as a catch-all category for patients who manifested multiple symptoms that fell between other diagnostic categories of mental disorders and were thus "on the borderline." BPD was thus in a sense a moving target. Only Multiple-Personality Disorder was more confusing to our customary ideas of human functioning and the two conditions may be closer than we imagine them to be under current diagnostic formulae.

Successive revisions of the DSM embody our changing views as to what is a mental illness and how it should be treated. Is BPD one disorder or a family of related conditions? Are Borderlines ill or merely difficult and contrary people? When does normal variation about a norm become an illness? Can a certain degree of dysfunction be presumed to apply to all persons? However these questions are answered, the presence of BPD draws attention to itself. The cyclonic affect storms or social withdrawal make demands upon others who cannot help but notice the distress experienced by the Borderline and the way that this distress is projected outwards in various accusations and demands made on other people.

The presence of BPD often elicits dismay and misunderstanding from those who do not suffer from its ravages themselves. What is this private tragedy being enacted year by year? Who is its author? What strange fate has condemned people who may possess such inner beauty at times to on occasion behave in a manner that even the person with BPD feels is embarrassing, tyrannical, or immature? Why is this diagnosis one that causes even professionals to draw a deep breath as if standing before a mountain that they must attempt to scale?

My answer is a simple one, because in the past no one understood what was going on and as a result was feeling about in the dark for a diagnosis when one lay in actuality close at hand. Borderlines are contradictory, challenging, and difficult because that is what BPD is. To face this head-on is to be already well on the way to overcoming it by ceasing to fight against the stream and to direct it instead. Those who suffer from Borderline Personality Disorder live in a mental state that makes impossible demands upon them. This in turn causes Borderlines to make impossible demands upon those who surround them. While holding other people to strict standards of behavior, Borderlines become accustomed (out of a perceived necessity) to granting themselves a wide divergence from those very standards as applied to themselves. What this means in practice is that Borderlines are difficult to be around and they know this at some level, but to live with themselves they project their feelings outwards upon other people. Repeated accusations often become the order of the day. Even people who love them are accused of all manner of failings and evil motives. This habit of inquisition and prosecution is relentless and it causes persons who must deal with Borderlines to establish within themselves a certain guardedness that can become a sort of "bunker mentality." Incoming mortar rounds are constantly to be expected. People who live with persons with BPD finally begin to experience a variety of Post-Traumatic Stress or Battle Fatigue. The habit of constant vigilance is so exhausting that it breeds a habit of constantly rehearsing words and actions for how they may be misperceived or distorted by the Borderline.

This double vision is often perceived by the Borderline as a further indication of duplicity and of inauthenticity which only confirms the Borderline's belief that people are not to be trusted. A Borderline will demand scrupulous honesty and then proceed to attack any resulting response. There simply is no safe ground.

Disappointing interactions mean that Borderlines are constantly engaged in managing damage control with promises that things will be better next time. This is because they fear abandonment which is a legitimate fear because many people, unable to bear up under the strains of the relationship, do in fact abandon Borderlines. This pattern of loss only confirms them in the suspicions that they habitually entertain about the world and about other people. Their pain may become unbearable and this in turn causes further acting-out and self-destruction.

The cycles of blame, violent outbursts, tears and regrets, and reunions chart the course of relationships with Borderlines. Their exquisite sensitivity to hurt and rejection does not prevent them from showing amazing callousness towards the feelings of others so that over time many people conclude that they are deliberately manipulative and dishonest rather than acting out of the desperation of the moment in what amounts to a sustained panic reaction to the demands of daily living.

The life of the Borderline is one of constantly attempting to prevent anxiety, depression, loneliness, identity diffusion, and the loss of self-esteem. The phrases "quiet frenzy" or "sustained desperation" come to mind as descriptions of the borderline state of being. Over years this habit of living becomes a global approach to coping in the world. A sort of me/them mentality makes Borderlines assume that everybody else has a secret way to manage life that they simply do not possess. It is like being under a curse that everybody else sees as self-indulgence or deliberate peevishness. The temptation is always present to say, "Why don't you just snap out of it." This of course is like asking a person with epilepsy to voluntarily control seizures. This is also why historically a BPD diagnosis was so disheartening. BPD was seen as an elective choice rather than the manifestation of a mental illness.

BPD is costly and limiting and not everyone is up to sharing the losses with the Borderline person and many persons with BPD end up alone. Object-relations Theory speaks of the Borderline's dilemma as that of lacking what is called object constancy. What this means is that the old phrase "out of sight out of mind" is uniquely applicable to how Borderlines feel about other people. When they are not actually present to correct misapprehensions various people in the life of the Borderline individual are subject to the corrosive actions of borderline fantasy. Small incidents can be blown up into hard data of evidence of betrayal or unreliability by the pervasive doubts that Borderlines entertain about their own self-worth when they are feeling depressed. When in a more exalted mood of omnipotence these same doubts are transformed into the suspicion of palace intrigues among the Borderline's courtiers. No one is quite what they seem to be and any sign of imperfection or inconsistency is presumed to be deliberate and malicious. Borderlines trust neither others nor themselves. The same inconsistency in their own concept of self is projected outwards into the world that surrounds them. Everything is always shifting about and resisting the desperate efforts to ensure stability and some measure of ego control by the borderline mentality. Emotional investments are therefore always seen as speculative and over time even long-term commitments are subject to periods of frantic "short-selling" as with a falling stock so that the Borderline will not be left abandoned and bereft. Loss becomes over time a self-fulfilling prophecy as they leave long strings of broken relationships behind them. Rather than see this as evidence of an improper life-strategy, Borderlines presume that it is evidence that they will always be victimized and misled whenever they care deeply about anyone. Isolation becomes a habit of mind and increasingly an actual fact in the life of the Borderline person.

As important people diminish over time there is a corresponding increase in the importance of place and circumstance. Order and control are exercised over objects which are less likely to rebel by asserting independent needs or desires in opposition to the willfulness or desperation of the person with BPD. Vast trains of interwoven associations make certain objects virtually talismanic as though containing magic energy to trigger memories. No incident is immune from being recalled in all of its manifestations and anything associated with an incident or person can invade various objects. These may themselves become infected by prior associations so that to lose them is to lose everything that has been embroidered into them in the vast and growing tapestry-shrouded world of those with BPD.

The intensity of their inner life is sometimes belied by an outer poverty of affect. Their desperate desire to be understood is motivated by a wish that others might learn something of the vocabulary and syntax of this private language of things and events. Much of the life of the borderline individual is occupied in repetitive performances of old scenes, always seeking some deeper meaning or way that events might have been prevented from unfolding as they once did, but since the past is not subject to erasure or unilateral reform these constant replays exceed normal regrets or mourning and become tortuous and pointless exercises of self-denigration or blame.

This is the source of much of the agony of suffering for persons with BPD. As impulsivity and suspicion work their havoc Borderlines assemble a vast array of disappointments in life. These disappointments are in turn likely to impinge and deform what remains of happy thoughts associated with various persons or places. As time goes on an ever-deepening shadow tends to eclipse their lives with mourning and regret. This trend in turn only increases the need that the Borderline feels to protect and sustain whatever has yet to succumb to the erosion that can claw rivulets of tears in the empty plain of daily life. Desperation yields to further desperation as each new hope proves to be premature and sullied by the failure to be reduced to a tolerable form and constancy and thus be made permanently reliable and accessible as needed to provide inner solace. Brick by brick the Borderline constructs her own prison where like Sleeping Beauty in her castle surrounded by thorns she sleeps and awaits a deliverance that she both desires and fears.

What unique perspective may a lawyer offer to understanding a condition that may lead to such disastrous life consequences? Lawyers are trained to develop certain habits of mind, among which is to seek ways to distribute losses in an effective and rational manner. Losses in life are inevitable and desired outcomes may be defeated by chance, by oversights, or by human folly and willfulness. If these losses over time are assessed upon those persons who are in the best position to avoid them not only is our sense of justice assuaged but it is customary to expect change to occur in a positive direction as costs are absorbed by the proper parties and means are devised to minimize loss.

As applied to BPD the most effective therapies will be those that can clarify the cause and effect relations between the way that a borderline person deals with life and provide more effective life strategies and tactics that are theoretically available to them. This means first to stabilize as far as possible the life situation of the borderline individual and then to set up a structure that will provide ongoing support while they are engaged in developing new coping skills that may gradually be made habitual.

Resistance will of course be encountered. Many borderline persons have spent much of their lives in trauma-inducing environments where trust and structure were absent. Many have learned to rely only upon their own resources to survive and to keep some sense of an integrated self. The rapidity with which many borderlines react to what they feel to be insults or betrayals stems from the intense fragility of their egos and their readiness to believe the worst about others and themselves. Many Borderlines have learned techniques of dissociation and isolation simply to survive. To ask them to surrender these techniques prior to discovering that a safer and wider world exists is to ask them for a faith that they do not yet feel able to profess. This means that mere insight into their dilemmas is usually insufficient to produce lasting change though these realizations may provide motivation to address their issues. Therapy must provide a safe environment for experimentation and integration of changes over time. In return for this promise the person with BPD must manifest acceptance and agree to a good faith effort to remain in treatment and to refrain from behaviors that will significantly undermine the therapeutic goals. Such actions may include substance abuse, continual efforts to alter the treatment protocol, or attacks on the process by acting-out or by a cynical questioning of the competency of the therapist or the potential efficacy of the treatment.

Borderlines seem to crave disappointment, as though hope itself was the most unbearable of pains. Much of the difficulty of treating BPD is the conviction of those who suffer from it that the world view that they initially present is correct. Borderline persons have often existed for years in intolerable life situations where they were neglected, abused, or ignored. Many people with BPD are remarkably sensitive and intelligent. They have not been able to connect with their surroundings in a mutually affirming way. Some have been made the scapegoat in dysfunctional family structures or may have simply encountered a string of particularly unfortunate life events that have led them to adapt borderline pathology as their best survival technique at that time and place.

Identity is the fruit of many interactions: change those interactions and personal growth will tend to follow. By placing the borderline person in a new and cohesive environment, adaptations in a more healthy direction will tend to occur. Therapy if it is to succeed must not be tangential but holistic. Factors that help sustain borderline behaviors must be removed and replaced by factors that support healthy changes by making them self-reinforcing and finally becoming part of a new definition of the self.

Lawyers learn that costs can be reallocated over time and that assets tend to migrate towards their optimum use. The same asset may be pursued by parties with conflicting interests each of which is asserting a claim of the exclusive right to possess it. Rights are by their very nature subject to question and dispute.

This means that the law is largely about resource allocation and the moral and rational convictions that lend support to compliance. Civilization demands compromise; thus the laws serve civilization by working towards mutual assent by the parties to various transactions.

Life must be re-negotiated on a daily basis. Personality disorders are caused by taking various life-stances that are too narrow and rigid to adapt to variable and changing circumstances. Therapy can help the borderline person to approach the world in a more open manner and to curtail impulsive efforts to impose a meaning on events or persons that is untimely or one that presumes consent simply because the borderline person would have it to be that way. As better means of negotiating with others and with their own emotions replace those used to ill effect in the past the patient will notice that many of the panic-driven responses that were formerly so natural will appear in all their unreasonableness and unsustainable nature.

Eventually BPD will be seen as just what it is: a violent and desperate attempt to bend the world to fit an inadequate model of the way that things are. Much of the mystery of BPD is dispelled by simply realizing that desperate people tend to do desperate things. Effective negotiation with the borderline personality means finding ways to lessen that interior desperation that has for so long characterized their dealings with the world and with their own perceptions. This requires empathy, support, and availability as new ways of dealing with life are encountered, found to work, and finally made habitual.

Until this stage is reached it is not too much to say that BPD can ravage lives. The chaos of borderline lives can act as a sort of moral vacuum that is waiting to be filled by various noxious experiences and entities. It is difficult enough to deal with the tasks imposed by daily living from a posture of basic honesty, respect for self and others, and a generally optimistic sense that progress can be made and talents can be usefully employed to achieve a balanced sense of well-being, mutually supportive relations with friends and associates, and to create an abiding sense that the world that we inhabit is basically responsive to our effort to create a civilization; but BPD predictably interferes with all of these by turning these presuppositions upside down. This reversal produces the cynicism of the disillusioned and the despairing.

Rather than a mood disorder, strictly speaking, persons with BPD live in a world of chaotic perceptions and impulses that are inordinately colored by a need to avoid psychological pain by taking desperate measures to manipulate their environment. To use a metaphor, the volume of their lives is turned up too high; everything is just too intense. The emptiness that they may feel at their core may be filled by being a victim to love affairs with partners that are borderline themselves or even sociopathic opportunists who will use and then discard them. The career of the daughter of Karl Marx, Eleanor Marx, provides an example of this tragic scenario in her relationship with the opportunistic con-man Edward Aveling. Another example is provided by the relationship between the poet and painter, Dante Gabriel Rossetti and his muse Elizabeth Siddal.

History contains many such examples of tragic dramas of the past that may reveal the presence of character pathology. Courts of law witness these events on a daily basis as criminal law attempts to impose some sense of order on events that have spun out of control. Deaths by suicide, families shattered, children abandoned, careers ruined by disgrace, what are these but a witness to the reality of evil among us? Modern psychology has attempted to abandon its use of what are termed "metaphysical concepts" as being beneath the dignity of a "social science." The law cannot afford this luxury. The repercussions of human actions set in motion forces that must be resolved or contained in some fashion. It is often the law that must accomplish this task. Literature is often the most fertile source to trace the origin and destiny of incipient motivations – of jealousy in Othello, of pride and the dishonor of age in King Lear, and of murder in the heart of Macbeth.

Universal human nature does not require endless statistical replication and the application of standard deviations to validate the human truths that re-emerge in every generation.

All human dramas have a moral core insofar as human nature is severed from the comparative innocence of the beasts. Tragedy requires the ingenuity and malice that only human beings display. If disastrous outcomes are to be avoided then stories must be told. Anecdotes may reveal a degree of wisdom and insight that more systemic studies have yet to reveal to those who claim to study the psyche or to probe the dim recesses of the soul.

The effort to appear dispassionate can blind us to the deeper meanings of life that the philosophers and poets did not hesitate to approach. Whoever reads Robert Burton's "Anatomy of Melancholy," will better understand depression and those who wish to understand various obsessive states will learn much from Fyodor Dostoyevsky. Wherever human conflict and confusion operate, the discerning mind can discover the wider dimensions of the drama of human moral choice and the suggestion of hidden sources of malignity or benefice. To abandon these dimensions of inquiry are as presumptuous as they are futile. BPD as a condition may be a disease of the soul as much as it is of the mind. Healing should be sought in a timely fashion from any quarter that may shed light upon an encroaching darkness before it claims its victims.

Chapter Three

Venom Magnets

The general impression left upon the lay reader after perusing various books on Borderline Personality Disorder is that even the experts are puzzled by the behavior and the nature of the inner world that is inhabited by borderline patients. It may not be too much to say that Borderlines possess or are possessed by a genius for suffering and chaos. They seem to be perpetually encased in a world of misfortune and regret. Mournful cypresses seem to grow naturally over their heads and melancholy ivy to twine its way along leaded casement-windows behind which they exist in a world of private meanings. To understand the borderline mentality is much like parsing a poem and it is not uncommon for literature to carry images and tropes that seem profoundly reminiscent of the experience of borderline patients who are caught in the octopus-like grip of their various set ideas and preoccupations.

Borderlines tend to brood over a simmering personal cauldron of past slights and present suspicions while weaving a dark shroud from their nights and days, one that casts a pall over past, present, and future. The operative question always seems to arise, "What will it take to make you stop all of this?" It is counter-intuitive to most people to seem to wish to make of doom a life-project and a destiny. Borderlines appear to be engaged in writing some vast tragedy of many acts to be performed before a theater of empty seats because most people are sufficiently engaged in their own struggles to have little time to enter the swift current of the Borderline's life. Many are reluctant to risk the conflict and confusion that will ensue if they become involved in a borderline person's secret and desolate world. After awhile (and incorrectly) many people reach the superficial conclusion that the Borderline enjoys his or her own condition.

It is true that a constant exposure to suffering can create a certain degree of dark pleasure in the power that can be exerted over others who may desire to engage in a quick rescue effort but over time Borderlines may become trapped in the quicksand of their own projections and false ideas. The script ceases to have an author and begins to write itself. Their own lethargy and lack of vision makes them prone to relapse into old habits rather than to challenge them by continuing in therapy. Ropes thrown down to them in the dark well where they languish are not grasped or are but feebly held. Anger and seeming ingratitude finally make outside efforts seem to be an imposition rather than a well-meant rescue attempt at all. Yet in spite of all of this resistance careful observers cannot avoid the conviction that beneath and in spite of all contrary evidence a healthy core personality, often one of startling radiance and beauty, is sending messages out into the stormy night from the foundering vessel where the borderline patient paces the deck that is breaking up beneath her.

It is through metaphor that it becomes possible to understand the world of the borderline individual. In the 17th century Robert Burton wrote his majestic early book of psychology entitled, "The Anatomy of Melancholy." His contribution has not exhausted the contributions that can be made to understanding BPD from sources that are literary in origin. Perhaps only character and symbol will ever be adequate to explain this puzzling condition. Psychology is after all the study of the psyche and it was precisely that study when ennobled by art that was the function of literature and it still is. The symptoms of BPD stalk about in various novels, dramas, and poetry and many great authors were perhaps themselves troubled by BPD. I need only mention "Madam Bovary," Heathcliff & Cathy in "Wuthering Heights," Ibsen's play "Hedda Gabler," and Miss Havisham from Dickens' "Great Expectations" to illustrate my point. Fiction can often embody what psychology can only name and statistically measure. Science is often in its communicative ability subservient to the creations of artists, musicians, and writers. These can convey mood in addition to meaning and it is in various moods broadly defined that we discover BPD.

Borderlines simultaneously loathe their condition and cannot effectively imagine another way of being. There is a facticity, a givenness about their lives that seems to deny the theoretical possibilities of human freedom. Phenomenological Psychology seeks to describe this inner world of the Borderline and those with similar disorders as one of being caught in time as in a trap and thus experiencing time as static rather than as what might be termed "rationally dynamic." By rationally dynamic I mean that process through which alternatives are weighed in the light of deliberately chosen objectives that are then pursued by allocating inner resources towards their achievement. In order for freedom to effectively exist there must be a sense that alternatives are possible and simultaneously there must exist what has been termed "the Élan Vital," which is that ongoing sense that time is not stagnant and intractable but is available to be filled through an active force that springs from within and from the source of life itself.

In contrast to this approach to existence Borderlines tend to experience the world as stagnant and frustrating and to experience their drives as intrusive demands that must be either recklessly consented to or ruthlessly denied. Life for someone with BPD is a constant battle with the ordinary demands of living. The achievement of moderation, balance, and control are difficult for Borderlines. Random acts of "freedom" take the place of selective choice and follow-through. Yet the ghost of responsibility still lingers within them and the result is experienced by borderline persons as a sense of pervasive shame and personal inadequacy to cope with inner conflict and the generalized indifference of a busy world.

This is why Borderlines so often seek out nurturing relentlessly so as to be able to internalize parts of the sustaining other, what psychologists refer to as "partial objects." The idealization of significant others by the borderline patient stems from her felt need to believe in the perfection of other people as a guarantee that this "split-off partial object" will continue to provide an anchor to existence since her own sense of inner imperfection makes her doubt that she can ever be adequately adult in her own regard. She may doubt that her own talents and resources are sufficient to resolve issues and to enable her to take responsible actions to fulfill her own realistic goals. Instead of goals of realistic achievement Borderlines often dream of a quick rebirth, a magical total fulfillment through love, or some dream of an earthly Parousia. Instead of seeking to find adequacy and satisfaction in an imperfect world, one that all of us share as we try and help each other and to forgive past offenses, Borderlines take an attitude of "take no prisoners" as they pursue either total victory or nothing. History denies that total victories are ever achieved by nations or civilizations much less by individuals. But disappointment need not equal despair and hope is our best collective guarantee that life will always triumph over destruction and the follies of humankind.

How does this dilemma of the stalled will that has been replaced by willfulness appear to other people? It may be presumed that the other party (or parties) to a contract arising out of what I term the Borderline Situation do not themselves suffer from BPD. It is necessary for these persons to understand the effects produced in their own lives by being exposed to behaviors of the borderline individual if progress is to be made and defensive measures against the various unpleasant scenes that often occur with Borderlines are to be effective. If the account in previous chapters explains what BPD is like from inside this chapter will attempt to explore how their chaotic manner of dealing with life appears to its distressed and puzzled witnesses.

No enemy will ever say the things that will be said by a raging Borderline. Other people are virtual magnets for borderline abuse and the degree of malice is directly proportional to the closeness that may have been achieved with them, often at great personal cost and over many years. This virtual emotional "liquidation sale" of accumulated esteem can be triggered by almost anything. At no time has one ever built up a balance of favors rendered, past atrocities forgiven, or pleas for forgiveness accepted to cover this sudden run on the emotional bank account. Bankruptcy is only a phone-call away and debts can be called in instantly, debts that one never even knew had been accruing interest in the account books kept in the dark vaults of resentment kept by every Borderline; the presumption that anything that they do is immediately remediable and worthy of being overlooked is coupled with an assumption that anything that the borderline finds displeasing in other people's actions or character is part of a well thought-out and nefarious plot against them. The Borderline concludes that at last the truth is out. She has been the victim of a well thought-out deception. Borderlines when in a rage do not have Napoleonic delusions of grandeur, Napoleon simply isn't sufficiently important in their eyes.

If nothing else the Borderline will condemn a person for being foolish enough to have trusted them. Fidelity will be the ultimate proof of desperation and hence of being unworthy of the Borderline's esteem. Few things in life are more likely to bring pain and sorrow in its train than to have any personal contact at all with a person with a diagnosis of BPD so to that degree the Borderline is correct. To love someone with BPD is risky to say the least.

So why stick it out with a person with BPD? The reason is that beneath their symptoms many Borderlines are among the most delightful, caring, and special of human beings. Borderlines can be creative, brilliant, and desirable. At some level they know this and exploit their charm over others, but like everything else about BPD the opposite disposition is never far away. The compulsion to ruin good things can seem at times to be perverse and willful rather than adventitious and traceable to their illness. The difference between BPD and other types of personality disorders is that Borderlines can appear to be saints who are possessed at times by an evil spirit. They are no more attracted to their less savory aspects than anybody else is. They may lament their variety of atrocious behaviors in the very act of engaging in them and yet perceive no real alternatives to exist.

Borderlines spend a considerable part of their lives engaged in mourning the past. Life appears to be an endless succession of broken relationships, legal difficulties, and hospitalizations. They may have been diagnosed with multiple illnesses before finally being cast into that vast holding cell called BPD where exasperated therapists finally put people who appear at times to be psychotic and at other times appear to be perfectly normal. Their often histrionic quality leads some people to believe that they are shamming when they report inner distress or panic.

The legal order often simply assumes that they represent a criminal type and Borderlines are often functionally lumped in with sociopaths. These most desperate of all sufferers of mental illness often end up on various borderlands where society puts its exiles in the hope that someone else will assume the costs of their maintenance and treatment. Since they often cannot contain their various conflicting emotions nor effectively restrain their actions they are perceived to be like a whirlwind or tornado that leaves a trail of damage in its wake. The hope for many people is that the storm will simply move along. But these are people after all and not blind forces. They are persons well worth salvaging. The problem is that any attempt to do so is likely to be resented because in the periods between their meltdowns or desperate acting-out behaviors Borderlines tend to assume that they are right and everybody else is wrong.

The key to BPD then is simply to assume that for the Borderline opposites will occur with the frequency of an alternating electrical current. Expect reversal and you are as close to constancy as you will ever get with an untreated Borderline. By reversal though I am not speaking of simply ordinary divergence of the estimation of a person's character; instead what must be expected is a frontal attack of such vehemence that any faults possessed will be portrayed the equivalent of an indictment issued by the War Crimes Tribunal at Nuremberg. Critique becomes nothing less than demonization. Only those who have experienced the rage, contempt, and viciousness of a full-scale borderline attack can comprehend its impact upon a person's well being. The words of Father Merrin in

Peter Blatty's novel, "The Exorcist," come to mind. As the two priests ascend the stairway to confront the possessed girl Father Merrin warns Damian that he should not listen. The attack is relentless and psychological and meant to destroy the self-esteem and confidence of the recipient of the attack. Damian is warned that the demon is a liar but that the devil will "mix lies with the truth to deceive us." Small faults or oversights will be condemned from the august height of Borderline pride as the greatest of personal failings.

Chapter Eight of this book talks about surviving when the Borderline throws people overboard and how to find a life-boat in time. The best thing of course is to never begin the voyage in the first place but to jump ship while the gangplank is still in place and while there are people on the shore to witness that the prospective passenger to Devil's Island has descended it to arrive back onto solid land there to lose himself as quickly as possible in the crowd while ignoring desperate pleas from the command deck to return to the ship. The next best choice is never to make a reservation to share the luxury stateroom of the Borderline's esteem; better to stay below decks in steerage. When dealing with a Borderline at each successive port of crisis the passenger fee must be paid all over again. If the benighted passenger has stayed on deck too long he must expect to be keel-hauled along the barnacle covered hull of the ship only to emerge in the wake as a bleeding wreck while the sharks of self-doubt and shame at being so readily victimized begin to gather for the kill. With luck friends will drag the passenger from the waters and rather than simply saying, "We told you so," they will be there to bandage wounds.

Recuperating after a romance with a Borderline is like the process of re-entry to the atmosphere of earth from the regions of cold interstellar space where like a space-shuttle he has been orbiting sometimes for years all along under the delusion that he was on an ocean voyage to the enchanted isles. These experiences, it is important to stress, give little pleasure to the Borderline herself. Any apparent victory only condemns her to a re-experience of her isolation and confirms her sense of herself as a victim by becoming a victimizer. The roles are finally interchangeable.

To suffer from Borderline Personality Disorder might be summarized as possessing the trait of a genius for misery. Borderlines draw to themselves all manner of misfortune. Cycles of betrayal and victimization make them seek paradoxical solace in various acts of self-abuse and when they are not abusing themselves they are engaged in ravaging the lives of others whom they perceive as threats or as persons who are about to abandon them. It is often as if Attila the Hun had a softer side and after burning and pillaging turned to the homeless villagers and cried piteously, "Why don't you understand me?" Borderlines seem to invite compassion only to scorn those who extend it to them. Demanding absolute compliance with their willfulness they will then blame their victims for being so foolish as to have believed them. Nothing is owed from them in return; no obligations of mutuality are incurred; the direction of benefits and understanding point to them alone.

Cycles of atrocities finally breed a habit of expecting advance absolution for anything that they might do. A Borderline will expect that anything is forgivable in their own conduct while holding others to the same standards as an Old Testament prophet dealing with the unconquered heathen tribes of Canaan. Giving time or love to a borderline person is like watching offerings being sucked into a black hole that does not allow even rays of light to escape. Voracious and implacable as salt-water crocodiles Borderlines think of themselves as ill-used by a universe that should be designed to gratify their every whim. Only the occasional signals flashed across the stormy sea of their lives like a message sent from a ship in distress as it nears the reefs of a lee shore calls forth any remaining desire to rescue them just one more time. As they are hauled to safety they are as likely as not to ask not for a blanket or a cup of hot soup but for the Captain's own cabin as only their just deserts.

The Borderline Personality structure in other words is one that accepts outrageous conduct and callousness as a sort of divine right of kings that applies to them alone. To anyone who has had close personal contact with a Borderline it is natural to wonder why they are not tracked by the CDC like some deadly virus and why quarantine measures to protect the public are not demanded and instituted. Averse to virtually any therapy they will alternately attempt to bend the therapist to their will before dropping out of treatment because "the therapy just isn't helping." Even an exorcist if consulted would probably say, "Pazuzu I could handle but this…!"

So it is that persons with BPD filter down the years like so much radioactivity bleeding into the soil from rusty drums at a nuclear disposal site. Their lives are a series of broken relationships, trips to the emergency room, serial attempts at getting therapy, drug and alcohol abuse, semi-intentional accidents, and various forms of institutionalization. And yet there is something within them behind this massive structure of defeat, selfishness, brutality, shallowness, and egocentricity that calls for help with the result that people keep offering it. There you have what is the Borderline Situation. BPD is a life-structure based upon a combination of victimization and forlorn hope. Impossible to tunnel in to where they languish and apparently impossible for them to tunnel out, various cries keep being heard on the surface in the open air where birds are singing and sunlight plays upon the flowers. There is clearly someone buried down there but how to reach them? That is the problem that has eluded all but a few attempts at devising an effective therapeutic approach for the treatment of BPD.

Could a legal analogy perhaps help to supplement therapy by first exploring the structure of the borderline situation and then setting up a contractual model for changing it? Transactional situations draw upon the unique skills of attorneys in clarifying objectives and embodying them in contracts with clear remedial options. As a shot in the dark it might just be possible to devise a type of reality-based therapy based upon stripping away the various types of camouflage employed by Borderlines in their guerilla war with the world.

The type of contract that I have in mind here is not confined to the therapist/patient relationship to create the therapeutic alliance that is necessary for psycho-therapy. What I am advocating is that *all persons* dealing with a person with BPD treat the relationship as conditional on good faith compliance by all parties and in process of ongoing negotiation.

The spontaneous quality of give and take in everyday social interactions simply presumes too much where the Borderline is concerned. Since interpersonal trust is almost certain to be absent, a better approach to people with BPD is one of fair-trade and negotiation to create mutual advantage in a bargained for exchange, what is often called an "arms-length" transaction. By making expectations clear and explicit to all parties to the negotiation a pattern of practice in contractual compliance can begin.

As patterns of successful transactions emerge the Borderline can experience what successful human relations feel like. Eventually broader definitions of terms can be accepted by both parties and justified reliance may allow a measure of trust and credit to be extended. In this way the disappointments and perceived betrayals that the Borderline expects to encounter may be reduced and more positive experiences may be substituted. This approach is forthright and honest and will hopefully end the pattern of the Borderline's search for a savior and the resulting disappointment and scorn when other people prove to be only human after all.

The splitting defense that is so common among persons with BPD is traceable to what might be called a strict-constructionist view of the way that the world operates. By presuming that they are fatally flawed Borderlines also presume that other people are withholding the vital life-force that the Borderline needs simply to cause them pain. "Why don't they understand me? Don't they know the pain that I am in? How can they be so callous? They must be evil!" This is the inexorable trend of borderline reasoning. From being a victim the person with BPD may suddenly go into attack mode. Once the other is defined as evil and one's own cause is seen as totally justified retaliation is considered to be not only just but even righteous. The problem is that the resulting purge or prosecution only drives other people away. Then when the surge of energy has passed the borderline rage like a fire that has exhausted its fuel turns on the Borderline herself and she begins to tear into her own flaws and inadequacies.

Even her own flesh may not be spared and in many instances it is then that impulsive self-abuse begins: cutting, reckless driving, substance abuse, binge eating, or various attacks on whatever friends she may still possess. Sometimes various precious objects may be destroyed. This desire to undo events in order to fix them somehow demands sacrifice, reparation, and pain from people with BPD as they try to exert control over the uncontrollable in themselves and in others. It is this pointless and detrimental cycle that must be stopped.

The first goal of treatment then, one that is a prerequisite for all further treatment, is to interrupt this insidious cycle of destruction. But in order to do this there must be an understanding of the causes of the highly emotional states that can be triggered in someone with BPD. If techniques of such as mapping and the use of flow charts were applied to trace the lightening-quick sequence of events that can be triggered by in effect putting the borderline thought processes into a slow-motion mode, then it could be seen that there is an inherent logic in borderline responses to stress or to any perceived neglect or devaluation shown towards them by significant others.

Once triggered the quality of all former relations is suddenly called into question by what is presumed to be proof of an unforgiveable oversight or a calculated incidence of treachery on the part of the other person. When the borderline alert system signals that the other party is wrong a sense of absolute justification comes into play and the relentless self-criticism of the borderline person is turned like the head of the Medusa towards the perceived malefactor. A take-no-prisoners order is sent out to the troops. The storm will rage until its crescendo is reached and the clouds part. It is only then that the person with BPD may look about her and seeing the wreckage on the shore she may begin to doubt whether she was correct after all. The deep and yawning abyss of self-doubt and shame returns to its relentless gnawing at her sense of self-esteem and her sense of internal security; the switch moves back from "attack and destroy" to "inner emptiness" and the relentless cycle of loneliness and desolation begins again.

An essential caveat here is that these abuse cycles are only partially within the control of the person with BPD. It is not uncommon for persons with BPD to suffer brief periods of reactive psychosis or paranoia when under stress. It will not be effective to map their responses, to negotiate, or to reason a Borderline out of a set of beliefs that no longer responds to reality testing. The rapid associational thinking and ideas of reference that may be present at such times allow the Borderline to assemble a simplified and ad hoc version of the way that things operate. A single central idea may fixate the attention and all contrary evidence will be seen as irrelevant. When this occurs it is best to defuse the situation as rapidly as possible. Often time and distance will restore perspective. It should be kept constantly in mind that any sanguine tone that I adopt in the exposition in this book on BPD is still up against the reality of severe pathology in borderline functions. To portray ideal outcomes is no guarantee of actually achieving them.

Chapter Four

A Contract Model

It must be stated at the outset that I am aware that contractual consent requires the ability to assess alternatives, to make a commitment in good faith, and to presumably fulfill the contractual obligations thus voluntarily assumed. None of this may be possible when dealing with a borderline individual. In fact their very illness lies in their instability and their constantly altering states of will. The approach of this book is for this reason less designed to be a statement of a practical reality for the Borderline than it is a way of structuring the goal-setting for those persons affected by living in the gravitational region of a person who may be engaging in unrelenting attacks and abuse against those whom the Borderline both needs and fears. It is my hope that this book may provide for these helpless bystanders a vantage point beyond the flames of the conflagration in which they are caught by virtue of relating to a Borderline person. If this can be kept in mind it will be possible to keep at least some outside bearings when dealing with the daily trials and tribulations that will lie ahead in relating to someone with BPD.

I am not the first to suggest a contract concept as applied to the treatment of BPD. My contribution here is confined to the application of negotiation to "the borderline situation" as opposed to personifying the issues raised by BPD. Negotiation implies a search for a middle-ground between two or more parties to the contract each of whom may be pursuing their own best interests. It is because many people who suffer from BPD appear to be deliberately and even willfully self-destructive that the negotiating parties may appear at times to be paradoxically negotiating on behalf of the perceived interests of the other party rather than their own. Even the "therapeutic alliance" is sometimes difficult to forge with Borderline patients. The situation must be analyzed as objectively as possible, as though it is the situation that must be explored not the persons involved who may be interchangeable. By abstracting from the dramatis personae and looking at the structure of the drama (and drama it often is) of the play it is possible to gain aesthetic distance and to visualize the mechanics of what is actually occurring. This allows for an objectivity that can quiet conflict and calm emotions that often run high in dealing with BPD. This tends also to diffuse the willfulness that leads Borderlines into isolation, impulsive actions, and symbolic gestures to act out their pain and to gain a sense of control by doing so.

Borderlines tend to be become fascinated by the process of their own unraveling as their lives traverse various ghastly regions on the way to ultimate ruin. There is a ritualistic quality to their displays of inappropriate affect and acts of private reparation through their own sacerdotal means. No Aztec altar smeared with blood can be more sanguinary than the dark halls of the Borderline mind echoing with brutal and cynical laughter. It is in hours such as this that BPD seems to cross over into actual metaphysical evil. It is to restore some sense of balance, proportion, and sanity that this contractual model is proposed.

Contractual relations in this world stem from the need to find some basis for enforceable expectations in a world of divergent interests. The process of reaching agreements is called negotiation with its attendant features of discussion and compromise. Without communication and at least some basis in shared meanings it is impossible to form contracts. Borderlines tend to push to extremes the notion of individuality and private interest. This is not mere selfishness on their part but is rather an ordinary and logical result of being a separate human being with a unique history.

In addition Borderlines tend to be stalled before the obstacles that are more readily surmounted by others because most people do not take time to realize the inherent contradictions that exist in daily life. Borderlines in other words seem to be more in touch with life in a manner that shows sensitivity, drama, and reflection. Their emotional extremes reflect a very real anguish and the misunderstandings that they encounter are crushing precisely because of a real inner innocence and vulnerability to rejection. The push and tumble of life in urban or anonymous settings can cause acute distress for them as they look about for affirmation and sympathy. Too much data or facts shorn of context and texture can grate on their nerves like nails across a blackboard. Everything is perceived as personal and intentional so that inadvertent slights particularly from those to whom they look for nurture or stability are perceived as betrayals or as callous and premeditated attacks. By combining extreme sensitivity to the behavior of others while being insensible to their own incursions or outrages when angry, frustrated, or afraid, Borderlines tend to alienate others and confirm their own sense of their profound difference and isolation. Borderlines enter negotiations with others at a disadvantage because of their often depleted resource base, a mistrust of other people, and a general aura that is perceived by outsiders as strange, bizarre, excessive, or suspicious. Low-tech verbal warfare suffices when other means are not at hand. Desperate circumstances and impulsivity lead Borderlines to play often very dangerous games with their lives and with the well-being and emotional integrity of other people.

Authority figures are often profoundly threatening to Borderlines and minor conflicts may appear to entail huge consequences that are disproportionate to the issues that are actually at stake. During a meltdown their entire world seems to be falling apart and it often comes as a surprise to other people when they hear what actually occurred what symbolic meanings the incident had for the Borderline. The rigid insistence on control that many borderline patients exhibit is due to the disorienting effect of others' proximity to the concentric circles of defense within which the Borderline establishes her defenses. Objects, space, and access are monitored so as to strain out in advance potential sources of chaos or threat. Monitoring distance – physical and emotional – is one of the main defenses used to keep a sense of control.

The all or nothing nature of borderline coping strategies may vary from impulsive recklessness to a hermit-like reclusiveness. Even ordinary tasks can seem insurmountable at times if they involve openness, uncertainty, or exposure. These response patterns indicate more than the mere effects of social anxiety or manifestations of obsessive shame. Nor are they strictly speaking signs of agoraphobia. It is more like what one might feel while orbiting in space if it was necessary to venture outside the containment vehicle of the space-ship. By monitoring their environment and packing their relationships in protective material like delicate vases Borderlines seek to avoid the twin dangers of flooding impressions that overwhelm their coping defenses and the desolation and emptiness that follows any perceived abandonment. The so-called de-compensation of Borderlines into psychosis overlooks the functionality of their inner meaning system and the symbolic and meaning-fraught nature of a borderline person's perceptual experience. What appears as mere irritability or moodiness in them is in reality a struggle of no small proportions to keep intense anxiety, shame, terror, or anomie at bay. Structure always serves some function even if that function is magical, symbolic, or excessive in terms of expended risks and resource depletion.

By approaching the Borderline's private world as one would approach a modern poem requiring a close-reading that proceeds line by line it is possible to see the underlying pattern of the life and the forces that piranha-like tend to lie in wait to ambush with doubts, qualifications, and a general bleeding away of her confidence. What is missing in persons with BPD is that general sense of content and security that most people tend to presume is the natural and consistent way of feeling about themselves and the world. Instead, borderline persons swim about in a stormy sea going from island to island where they may rest for a time and regain their strength before pushing off once again into the raging waters. In less dramatic language this mental state is spoken of as one that is lacking in object constancy. Many of the diagnostic criteria of BPD stem from actions that the Borderline person takes to negotiate a passage through life while lacking the central core of secure perceptions and stability of self and confidence in others that most people take for granted.

By defining BPD as more than mere personal pathology I am deliberately locating the problem in the interpersonal world of contemporary living where it is most manifest. Phenomenological psychology refers to this as the Mitwelt, the world of relations that lie between people, our shared existence. The social component of life provides the inner world with its points of reference. We continually integrate partial portraits of others into ourselves just as object-relations psychology teaches. We assemble a self out of the elemental experiences of reward or punishment that life exposes us to in the case of significant others and fundamental relationships. These partial-objects become in time disembodied voices, ghosts of the past that speak through our mouths their unlived motives, aspirations and disappointments. We shift continually between various states of being and call forth skills, gestures, and aspects of ourselves to meet various challenges. Persons with BPD often lack the ability to smoothly transition through the various conflicted elements of their personalities. Often the tools are simply inadequate and this causes embarrassment and shame. Exposure is dreaded, withdrawal begins, and the doors to the Mitwelt are closed.

The oriental family recognizes that the spirits of the past demand sustenance from the present generation. The traumas and discontents of all whom we have ever loved and sometimes been wounded by live within us and write whole scenes of our personal dramas. Each of us is a haunted house and down the corridors of our minds there wander the spirits of our partial and incomplete life-scripts, many of which are not even our own. The seeds of the sacrifice of today may have been planted in another soul, another time, or a foreign land. Thereafter they have been passed on in a word, an expression, or a gesture that has been repeated often enough to become a habit of character. We read our fate in the tea leaves of a mother's smile or a father's disapproving frown. To bring to consciousness what has happened to form character, to connect the chains of the remote causes of personality is the task of psychotherapy with the Borderline. Insight is the goal and moderation and control are the desired outcomes. The field of our being is scouted and the areas from which ambushes may be mounted are mapped. It is only then that we begin to realize that much that we presumed was spontaneous and willed in our actions has really been a re-enactment of the macabre dance of the long dead people who were our progenitors.

All of this may sound quite mystical and the pragmatism in American psychology depends less on understanding than it does on outcomes. This is why experimental and statistical studies are so fascinating to American psychology. Words are essentially ambiguous and metaphor is even more so. Besides as a lawyer it may seem presumptuous of me to probe into the sacred precincts of the soul or psyche. For this reason it is advisable that I not stray too far into foreign ground and confine my observations to relations and not entities.

This book begins with the assumption that a different outcome than tragedy is achievable for those with BPD or at the very least that the Borderline's situation can be clarified so that all parties know what is at stake in relating to a person with BPD. By using the word "situation" rather than adhering to a depth psychology model I am hoping to avoid the endless quest for what underlies BPD, whether it is due to a disruption in object-relations, simply a learned set of inadequate responses to the world, or due to biochemical causes, genetics, or brain morphology. After all, lawyers deal with situations rather than hidden motivations. What cannot be backed up by evidence is either irrelevant or inadmissible because it is prejudicial rather than probative. So it is that I will attempt here to define borderline symptoms in an operational context and then ask what consequences are likely to follow from different inputs. This is what I mean by mapping – to create linkages that will allow the person with BPD to explain the steps between the input of an unpleasant affect at one end and the output of a maladaptive solution at the other end. By interrupting the chain new outcomes can emerge.

The most effective contracts are those that anticipate contingencies and spread the risk of losses when they occur. Contracts are future oriented rather than preoccupied by past conditions or harms suffered. The task is to locate borderline pathology in space and time, to identify the key players or stakeholders in the Borderline Situation, and to prepare the clauses of the contract with remedial options in case of breach. These remedies should not be seen as punishments but as the logical results of chains of causation. This robs them of much of their numinous quality, the very qualities that are over-freighted with anger and fear in persons with BPD.

There are of course objections to this approach. The first and most obvious problem with this approach is that Borderlines by definition are so changeable and impulsive that the capacity to agree to keep the terms of a contract is questionable at best. What this means is that the contract to be formed must be written so as to be somewhat one-sided in that it will have a bias towards healthy functioning as opposed to the usual modes of distress and danger that are the customary tendencies of positions taken by the borderline individual. In the beginning the contract may seem more like a traditional interpretive analysis; if this, then that. Insight is often less than immediately helpful when dealing with persons who are accustomed to use denial as a defense. Repeated linkages however can finally be appropriated and become elements of a formal "contract" used in the therapeutic context advocated here. Since the bargaining positions are not usually equal it should be pointed out that the person with BPD has much to gain and very little to lose by taking the risk of healing. The old way of life is always there waiting if the patient wishes to return.

The Borderline Situation is not strictly confined to the "identified patient" however. BPD does not emerge in a vacuum. Other people contribute their own dysfunctions to its nurturance, or if better habits are put in place to the dismantling of the syndrome. The person with BPD can get better. To an extent then the Borderline is a third-party beneficiary of all of the contracting parties whose interactions with the Borderline have heretofore enabled various manipulations that have not been in the patient's best interests to prevail. To not contribute to the disorder is of course to risk the wrath of the Borderline who cannot imagine what a non-borderline life-style would even look like. Any loss of control triggers panic in persons with BPD. The often mentioned defense of splitting is used to great effect to banish anyone who will not bow to the rigid world-view of opposed absolutes in which the Borderline customarily resides. A constant "war on terror" is being conducted but the terror is within the Borderline herself. The rush from one source of solace to another is unending. This accounts for the frenzied quality of life with a person with BPD.

Everything is a matter of life or death. Minor disappointments become major betrayals. Executions are always immanent even for relationships of longstanding. Borderlines are always building new bridges only to blow them up. Loyalty, longevity, and perseverance are supplanted by deep resentments towards significant others. Painful scenes are followed by self-loathing exercised towards the self. These doubts must be squelched at once to prevent a descent into an emotional abyss so Borderlines constantly review the files of old cases seeking justification in their own eyes as just one more case of a failure to measure up to the swift idealizations that constitute the other side of the mountainous terrain of the Borderline's world. There are no easy declivities into serene valleys in the case of BPD but only swift plunges from giddy precipices into ghastly abysses. The result is that anyone who deals with a Borderline had best keep a safety-line to other climbers and carry plenty of oxygen in the rarefied air.

To negotiate a contract with a party who will make few concessions unless forced to do so is not an easy task. It will help though to point out that the very reason for a contract is to attain what the law calls the benefits of a bargained-for-exchange. Exchanges occur so as to place each party to the contract in a better position than they were in prior to the agreement. The problem is that most Borderlines are accustomed to untrammeled success in getting their way because the means that they habitually use on others are so extreme, relentless, and brutal. Borderlines think little of risking everything on one throw of the dice. This explains why they often court accident and death, anything rather than compromise their intense willfulness or seriously consider another mode of living as possible for them. "My way or the highway" is their mantra. This is because trust/mistrust is the primary Borderline issue.

For these reasons I propose a contract as the best practical way of relating to a person with BPD because contractual terms can be specific and not based upon reliance upon the character of the other or any idealized projections. Contracts demand performance of the terms of the contract or damages for breach, one or the other. It is not because this technique is perfect that I suggest it but because so few other alternatives seem to succeed. To ask for a change of heart in a world-view that is as adamantine as that of the Borderline is unrealistic. Given time the sheer odds of continued risky behavior is unacceptable to anyone who cares about a person with BPD. This means that cause and effect must be clarified in the Borderline situation as soon as possible and then so linked that maladaptive behavior brings instantaneous and reliable feedback that opposes the borderline person's will towards destruction.

This does not mean punitive consequences in the usual sense because many Borderlines thrive on punishment and pain. The feedback I am talking about is negative only in the sense that it frustrates the unbridled willfulness of the Borderline or disarms a favored technique of manipulation. Far from being an exercise in so-called tough-love the approach that I am recommending is real love. Borderlines always tend to pair pain and love as being inseparably linked and distrust any love that appears to be disinterested and unselfish. By locating the point of change in the situation as opposed to the person the Borderline is spared the sense that she is flawed, shame is not awakened, and objectivity eventually becomes possible. Borderline panic is over time supplanted by confidence and trust in the course of the contractual performance of all parties.

One last major difficulty with this contractual approach to relations is that all parties to the Borderline situation need to be identified and made aware that they tend to feed the process of the illness by years of conditioned assent to the willfulness and threats of the Borderline. Self-esteem issues in caretakers are omnipresent. This may even necessitate a change in the initial treatment period of key people in the life of the Borderline because too many contaminants remain from past habitual behaviors of cooperation with the demands made upon them by the Borderline. This is why brief in-house periods of treatment are sometimes necessary as opposed to out-patient care. The important thing is to make it clear to all parties that a new day is dawning.

The radical change from compliance to gentle opposition that I am recommending will not go down easy with anyone who has lived for years in the Borderline Situation. It may even require a change of scene or hospitalization for in-house treatment to create a new life environment for the Borderline. But a change of skies alone will never suffice because borderline pathology constantly works to recapitulate the same outcomes over and over again. This means that less than ideal conditions must sometimes be accepted either because resources are scarce or because a lack of sufficient persons exist to create an adequate support system to endure the strains that the Borderline will predictably impose. Years of poor adaptation and paradoxical reinforcements must be reversed for recovery to occur.

Change requires a new set of inputs plus persistence over time. Setbacks and regressions must be followed by swift return to the path of healing. New pleasures must supplant the swift transitions between extremes that Borderlines have become accustomed to experiencing as the price of existence in an unstable world. Changing these perceptual givens takes time to engrain new patterns of expectation and response. How this can be accomplished will be the subject of the next chapters.

Chapter Five

Mapping the Hurricane

What I am calling "The Borderline Situation" has been the unfortunate result of a team project. The Borderline cannot weave her noxious web by herself. The web must be anchored at significant points of dysfunction. Mapping the situation requires identifying those points and the people and relations that are central to the dark drama of a borderline person's existence. Just as hurricanes can be studied as more than being simply chance disasters by mapping their origin and progress, so can the conditions that allow borderline dysfunctions to form and to ravage lives unimpeded. It is not productive to decide whether it is the Borderline or those who surround them that are most responsible for the ensuing havoc. Assignment of guilt and blame is less important than intervening in a situation that in its destruction and mindlessness damages all in the proximity of BPD. Just as the direction of a wildfire can change suddenly and put firefighting crews in danger, so can the acting-out patterns of borderline persons create anxiety and depression in others. Each of these metaphors captures some of the aura of threat, immanent disaster, and potential harm that those who have dealt with BPD have described.

It is important to recognize that no person is synonymous though with their symptoms or diagnosis so the discussion above must be confined to the illness which in the case of BPD has a profoundly aggressive component that can harm or endanger other people. Judgment of the illness and the need to adopt protective measures is no condemnation of the person who suffers from BPD. The patient herself usually suffers more intensely from her illness than other parties can imagine. By describing BPD as a blind force it is possible to remove some of the outrage that is felt when seemingly competent and responsible people with BPD behave in cruel and inhumane ways.

Hurricanes are produced when the energy of a low pressure system develops as a circular motion about the eye of the storm. The longer that a hurricane remains at sea before landfall is made the stronger it grows. Something similar occurs with persons with BPD. The longer the various strategies that the borderline person tends to adopt are allowed to continue unaddressed the stronger these dysfunctional patterns become. The task then for therapists is to intervene as early and as decisively as possible in the course of BPD.

Therapy with a person with BPD may be compared to deep-sea fishing. Picture a line with a marlin thrashing about at the end. The goal should be to allow no slack to develop in the line. When the fish runs it should be allowed to do so but with as much drag on the line as possible to tire the fish. When the fish turns and returns towards the boat it is important to take in the slack quickly. The analogy breaks down in one respect. Unlike the marlin the tumultuous sea in which the Borderline is drowning is not her natural environment. These waves of conflict and confusion bring the Borderline individual even less pleasure and joy than anyone else. A tight line means definite standards of expectation and behavior contractually negotiated and enforced on all parties to the contract.

To return to the hurricane analogy: once a hurricane begins to form at sea the task for people on shore is to prepare for its landfall and if they are at sea to get out of the way of the storm. Just as various map coordinates will describe the location and strength of the storm, various characteristics have been mapped out that Borderlines tend to exhibit. Once a diagnosis is made it should be possible to further sub-divide these characteristics as they individually manifest themselves in each patient's unique version of BPD.

By developing a list of highly personal coordinates based upon specific life-events it will then be possible to chart the course that BPD has taken thus far in a person's life and to analyze what factors have been in play to allow these painful incidents to manifest themselves. Past events cannot be changed of course but causal factors can be traced and alternative scenarios imagined. Events often allow for differently shaded interpretations. Even mistakes can teach us something. This is what it means to chart the course of the storm – to assess its strength, its past course, and likely direction.

Now let us return from these various analogies to the question of contract. Just as contract law ideally seeks to maximize the good for all parties in the bargained-for-exchange and to identify potential problems and conflicts before they occur, our BPD storm mapping specifics should provide potential areas for inclusion in the contract. It should be possible to imagine remedial actions that may spring into effect when triggered by specific events. The central problem of course is to secure commitment and compliance on the part of the person with BPD to the contractual terms. Discussion should be specific and the person with BPD should be asked to contribute ideas and to take a significant role in the negotiations.

Borderlines tend to resist any surrender of a measure of control because to do so requires trust and they are incapable of sustaining relationships requiring sustained trust. This means that there must be some degree of compulsion in the situation but the contract must finally receive assent to be effective. Escape routes must be seen as more obnoxious to the person with BPD than to consent to the terms of the contract.

This is where life comes into play. Borderlines have been playing a dangerous game with death, often for years. During this time they have developed an unreasoning confidence in their own omnipotence. Convincing themselves that life is so dreadful and untenable that they can afford to treat death as a friendly option has become a habit of their daily by-the-skin-of-their-teeth survival. Meanwhile outsiders are indifferent or perplexed and those who care about people with BPD are dismayed, angry, and powerless to alter the course of the slow motion train-wreck of the life of the person with BPD. Only by altering the pre-conditions that make such a way of life possible can any possibility exist of de-railing the Borderline's train ride to oblivion.

The contract as I have stated above may be a series of similar agreements on a common theme of recovery. It is not simply with the Borderline but with all persons involved in the Borderline Situation so that there is no "leakage around the seams" of the containing environment. Far from being a prison that targets the borderline patient this mutuality and cooperation among significant others prevents the Borderline from the manipulation which is one of the key components of her illness one that allows her to remain dysfunctional.

There is a need among people who deal with Borderlines for mutual support as they address the various crises to which Borderlines are subject. A team approach prevents the overload that can occur when one person is targeted by the borderline patient for abuse or rejection. Borderlines instinctively seek out the weak-link in a chain, the vulnerable wall in the citadel, and try to co-opt resources and good-will amongst any therapy team. It takes a united front to oppose the cunning strategic moves of the Borderline who feels compelled to constantly test and verify the good motives of others by sounding out any flaws or personal weak points that she can find.

Anything and everything that may provide a leverage point should be identified and made contingent upon compliance with the terms of the contract. The scope for further acting out should be constricted until, to return to the fishing analogy, "the fish is swimming around in a bucket." If this seems extreme it should be born in mind that some form of exterior containment is what borderline persons secretly crave because their experience of life has been of one vast and empty plain without guide or signpost. Part of their notorious changeability is the futile search for some sense of directionality, some compass points to limit and direct their boundless willfulness.

Even here though there are grounds for caution. Exceptions are discovered to every rule. Therapy is not entrapment but consensual. Only in the case of immanent danger to self or others should a person with BPD be confined. Rather, it should be pointed out that therapy is a sanctuary on a stormy sea, a harbor long-sought for that is just around the next headland. If the idea of containment and limit setting might at first appear to be contrary to the ultimate goal of psychotherapy, which is to strengthen the legitimate ego boundaries of the person with BPD, it must be recalled that it may take years to break the habits of perception and expectation that have been built up over a lifetime in the person with BPD.

Since the life experience of the Borderline has often been one of enmeshment or abandonment by significant others it would appear above all else to be important to treat the Borderline as an adult and to honor their choices even when those choices appear to be contrary to the borderline person's best interests, but in the short term empathy and artificial stability may need to be instilled from outside the patient much as a splint may help to support a broken bone during healing.

Even after entering such a contract BPD will seek to regain its victim. Borderlines seek out weak points compulsively. If optimists sort through piles of manure searching for the pony, Borderlines can sort through gold looking for any sign of leaden slugs. Every joy is held to be temporary or counterfeit and every love is tainted by potential betrayal or by assumed self-interest. Life is always filled with lemons for someone with BPD. By mapping out the unique coordinates of each Borderline individual's patterns of destruction it is possible unlike in the case of hurricanes to hasten the storm's landfall where restored to earth the storm may exhaust itself at last.

Borderline persons by definition appear to lack the internal resources and stable structures that are necessary to dispassionately weigh choices and to refrain from impulsive and chaotic actions. It is not uncommon for them to appear to thrive under pain and self-induced dramas that seem to appear spontaneously out of nowhere like a squall on a sunny day in tropical waters. Communication with a person with BPD requires an ability to follow the subterranean streams of their doubts, suspicions, fears, and general mistrust of other people. Borderlines are always testing the waters of even well-established and long-term relationships to seek out what they assume are the hidden fault lines that may produce future earthquakes and upheavals.

Borderlines presume that unfavorable outcomes are virtually inevitable and they seem to gain a feeling of power and control by appointing themselves as prosecuting attorneys toward a universe of persons and situations that are dedicated to their ruination. Then with lightening-like rapidity they may fear abandonment and heap all of the blame for what has just occurred back upon their own actions as positive proof of their inner badness and the well-deserved rejection and isolation that they both assume and presume is their ineluctable fate. It takes constant reassurance to convince the borderline individual that ambiguity and conflict are inevitable in human life and that relationships demand a degree of give and take and a sharing of strengths and weaknesses between vulnerable and imperfect human beings. Terminal uniqueness is not required in order for them to exist; they may join the human race after all.

Until this point is reached however, it is advisable to adopt a surrogate who will listen and gently correct misapprehensions by providing the ego stability that the Borderline does not possess on her own. This "sounding board" function of a therapist is virtually a prerequisite if the meltdowns are to be avoided that often occur when anxiety, anger, or dread makes the world of the Borderline temporarily overwhelming for her. These affect storms can be reduced to mere squalls rather than full-blown hurricanes if communication takes the place of panic-motivated acting-out behaviors. The need for empathetic mirroring makes later gradual exploration of alternatives possible. Regression to dependency should not be a permanent posture but it does make it possible to weather the storm and to make some gains as the tides of wind and wave recede.

In times of comparative calm and after at least a degree of trust has been established it should be possible for the Borderline to help in identifying triggers and sensitive zones that tend to evoke automatic and habitual acting-out responses based upon past experience. It is not uncommon for people with BPD to carve out a vast arena of exceptionalism and entitlement so as to negotiate with the world on the extreme terms demanded by their stringent and demanding needs. This causes their advent upon any scene to demand immediate adjustments by others and explains some of the outrage vented at those who suffer from BPD by other people and the social isolation that they may experience. The Borderline in turn feels misunderstood and hurt, assuming that other people are simply callous and unfeeling whereas they are in reality often guarding themselves from the powerful force-field put out by persons with BPD who often appear sarcastic, bitter, angry, or manipulative by turns as they seek to get their own way in any situation.

When their needs are not met Borderlines often experience great shame and guilt at recalling their previous demands and go from blaming others to castigating themselves and engaging in various self-punitive acts. This swinging pendulum between mutual contradictories might be the most indicative individual symptom that BPD is present. Caught between entitlement as a queen and exile as an outcast waif, between overweening pride and devastating self-contempt and mourning, the person with BPD spends her days and nights as puzzled by her own drives, obsessions and compulsions as others are (with the proviso that she often feels that she is the conscious cause and agent whereas BPD is in many ways an independent complex of behaviors and attitudes, and beliefs that though subject to insight and gradual correction are not strictly speaking under complete voluntary control of the person with BPD).

The purely physiological aspect of neural pathways is continually teaching us that the simple assumption of voluntary change to meet any contingency is unrealistic and subject to the refutation of experience. Only repeated efforts can form new habits and change character and even this may require outside support to be established. To simply drive symptoms underground only adds a habit of duplicity to painful affects allowing the unmapped regions of the mind to remain in obscurity. If instead of seeking a spurious repose in denial, common patterns are mapped and patterns of maladaptive or impulsive responses are replaced by delay, re-evaluation, and consideration of alternative coping methods, persons with BPD may make progress over time to more adaptive functioning, tolerance of disappointment, and confidence in their ability to weather their frequent emotional squalls.

In concluding this chapter I would   like to recall to the reader the subtitle of this book, "a lawyer looks at borderline personality disorder." To take a look at something is to imply a degree of subjectivity and it is for this reason that I have had to reach into my own analogies as tools for what I am attempting to describe. Candor demands that I remind the reader of this source of personal bias and to point out that lawyers have a penchant for disclaimers.

What I term a "refracted view" depends upon subjectivity. The study of BPD should not in my opinion be confined to mental health workers alone. There is a real sense in which lawyers are counselors with their own unique perspectives on human experience. To that degree a lawyer need not hesitate to explore human consciousness as I am doing here, even in the troublesome case of Borderline Personality Disorder. As for my penchant for marine metaphors and analogies drawn from the sea, well that is autobiography and need not concern us here.

What is important is that lawyers seek to find the intersections of conflict, human motivation, and attainable ends. Lawyers are, ideally speaking, facilitators of human goal-seeking behaviors. If BPD can be conceived as a poor life-strategy to pursue, one based on false premises that yield inadequate results, then a lawyerly way of approaching the issue may be of help to clarify the issues and even suggest some solutions.

Chapter Six

Separation of Issues

As the last chapters have explained, once the factors that make the Borderline Situation possible are identified it is possible to frame life events in a cause and effect context where results follow swiftly and reliably if not always with complete predictability or proportionality from causes. It is no longer possible for the Borderline to continue her desperate bargain against fate. Instead life is restored to its reality. Suddenly perceptions are revealed for what they are: partial viewpoints that must be tested by experience rather than representing alternately promises of paradise or gateways to hell. Ambiguity and disappointment are re-integrated as normal experiences of imperfect people in an imperfect world. Forgiveness takes the place of lashing-out and revenge in the Borderline's repertoire of responses. The binge and purge style of all-or-nothing is succeeded by rationing and budgeting of responses. Suddenly, balance appears to be a real possibility in the life of the person with BPD.

Because some degree of acting-out in BPD is inevitable and foreseeable it is essential to recovery to identify specific triggers and to evolve alternative responses to be deployed during times of relative calm. These alternative responses provide the terms of the contract. Even then failures may occur at times and when they do it is essential to find order and restitution again by applying the goal of liquidated damages clauses. These are less concerned with blame than with rebalancing the situation. Liquidated damages are so foreseeable that no special evidence is required to prove their appropriateness. A contract with a Borderline should specify what will occur when destructive acting-out happens in order to restore order. No longer will BPD behavior be granted the carte blanche of instant forgiveness or enabling. The Borderline will need to pull a weight of predictable inconvenience and reparation exacted for what were formerly wars-of-choice.

The momentum of events requires distance and time to achieve its ends so harms must be minimized by restricting the time and space available for wrong directions to advance and by a sustained policy of disarmament of the borderline person's favorite weapons of choice. Simple vibration in place is unsatisfying to Borderlines who love to anticipate a summer campaign with tanks rolling unimpeded towards the Volga. It often takes a Stalingrad to stop them. The best way to avoid this result is to provide a contractual provision that will let them "return to Berlin" by easy stages and pursue peace negotiations with some remaining dignity and sovereignty intact rather than to risk a mental hospital, incarceration, or premature death just to save face.

The contract form that I propose is one that involves helping the Borderline translate the flood of her impressions that often overwhelm her into more orderly channels of reliable and mutually validated human communications. Borderlines often experience the world in private symbols that carry an enormous load of private meanings that they assume that other people share or are at least aware of. It is possible to deeply wound a borderline person by a chance remark that trespasses upon a hidden forbidden zone or ignores an assumption that the Borderline has made. The contract in question then may require constant clarification of terms. In fact interpretation is of the essence in treating BPD. As such it is hardly surprising that when people speak in different emotional languages that disagreements and unintentional damage can occur. The task of effective communication requires persistence and insight followed by more persistence and even deeper insight. Good will on all sides will make this process easier. New beginnings then are the order of the day when dealing with BPD.

Since Borderlines are easily discouraged and accustomed to assigning blame readily it may take time to adapt to a viewpoint that is less concerned with assigning responsibility than it is in sharing it with another as part of a team. Each party to the contract can make good on the losses of the other in the imperfect battles of daily life by allowing some flexibility to exist in interpretation in the interests of keeping the contract as a whole viable. Memory can eventually be other than like an unruly washtub; one filled with regrets and resentments. It may become possible to carry along various unpleasant memories of past events with forgiveness and with grace.

The contract form that I am proposing may take many forms. It may take the form of "if this … then this." Consequences can be specified and their invoking behaviors described with some specificity. This is possible because Borderline acting-out usually follows a predictable course even though triggers may vary. Another possibility for the terms of the contract may prescribe rewards for positive actions or for actions that challenge existing fears or avoidance behaviors. The only form of the contract that will probably be of only marginal value is an unsupported promise to do better without specifying a time, place, or manner of action. Mere resolutions provide no guideposts for change or measuring criteria. Since Borderlines often behave as if they are different people at times even if they are not multiples the promises of one ego-state may not be transferable to the more destructive aspects of their personality.

For this reason Borderlines should not be pressed to commit to more than they may be reasonably expected to perform. Short term contracts of 30 days may be the outside limit of initial contracts. It is more important to succeed at small tasks than to anticipate long flights rather than glides in the initial periods. During this time the contracting parties will learn more about the private interior world of the Borderline and lists of triggers can be assembled. Exposure to anxiety or guilt-producing triggers should be gradual. Borderlines can be quickly overwhelmed by emotional flooding through small apertures. Their lightening-fast responses may similarly overwhelm therapists who may be well out on a minefield without realizing it. For these reasons contract terms should be severable and failure to keep one promise need not reflect on the enforceability of the remaining terms of the contract.

It should always be born in mind that my use of the term "contract" as used here is not a legal one but rather a metaphorical use of a legal term in a clinical setting. The point is to clarify communications by offer, negotiation and discussion, and finally acceptance. By having a written memorial of the agreement it is possible for both parties to point out the terms of the agreement and the surrounding history of its formation and any discussion that preceded formal commitment. There is a valuable formalism in actually manifesting assent by more than verbal assurances, which are often made by Borderlines under duress or as a result of panic to silence opposition or to prevent abandonment.

The terms of each individual contact must be preceded by identifying instances that trigger Borderline symptoms and pairing them with alternate courses of action that are more productive. These will then provide alternatives to be agreed upon by all relevant parties to the daily transactions with the Borderline. Situations that cannot be adequately identified in advance should be governed by a general agreement to suspend any Borderline acting-out until things calm down and the situation can be added to the terms of the contract.

The period that the contract is in force may be as short as three days or a week to be followed by a new contract negotiation in case of emergencies. Each preceding period can then be examined for lessons learned by all parties and the terms amended in the light of these lessons. The goal is a more comprehensive contract and one to be in force for longer periods of time. The contract metaphor is meant to make actions and reactions visible and to prevent the conceptual slide to which Borderlines are often subject.

Borderlines often speak an internal language with great logical jumps. Feelings tend to predominate over evidence and generalization from single instances is common. Whole trains of thought can be linked together and sent out into the world from tiny stimuli. Tracing a train of thought back to its origins in an off-hand comment can be quite enlightening as to the inner world of the Borderline. This is why denial or explanation is usually pointless. Borderline logic is intuitive, rapid, and emotionally charged with past instances that may have nothing to do with the person at hand or the circumstances of a present interaction. The fall of a piece of eiderdown may sound like an avalanche or a firecracker may be reduced to a mere whisper. Linkages are vague or so personal as to be incommunicable. Add to this a rapidity of response and an inability to contain emotions in the short-term and it can be grasped how difficult it often is to negotiate terms once an emotional free-fall has begun.

The parachute of the Borderline Contract must be prepared therefore during those times when comparative calm reigns and some degree of objectivity and cooperation on the part of the Borderline may be presumed. The next chapter will discuss what should be done when Borderlines enter periods of regression or severe acting-out when they are incapable or unwilling to adhere to prior commitments and return to testing the therapeutic or other relationship by extreme actions or words. Borderlines appear to be compelled to court abandonment and isolation whether to punish themselves or to expose the vulnerabilities of other people. Borderlines tent to pursue the goal of an elusive "gold standard" in a world of paper currencies. So great is their fear of the variability and contingent nature of life that they often prefer a definite failure to gradual improvement and partial satisfaction. In fact it is to gradually wean them away from their abiding "total approach" to life that therapy must be primarily addressed. Borderlines seem to sustain their balance by rushing back and forth between opposites rather than making minor adjustments from the middle-ground. The first step then is to convince them that such a middle-ground of ambiguity and stability exists and then to give them lived experience of what it feels like to dwell there for gradually lengthening periods of time.

As familiarity increases the person with BPD will come to believe that this zone of comparative safety may be accessed by various self-soothing methods and that other people, though not perfect or uniformly available at all times, still do care about them and are doing what they can within their own limitations, the same limitations that all human beings share by virtue of being human. To end the phenomenology of exceptionalism that makes people with BPD presume that they are drifting about alone on a frigid ice-flow abandoned in an arctic sea is already to take a step forward into a brighter region of human existence.

Shame is the primal sense of exposure and persons with BPD often adopt a sustained posture of defensiveness against others for fear of displaying those very conditions that define us as being human. The ordinary becomes problematic when it has been defined as something that can be eluded rather than being faced as one of the constant adjustments that life demands of us all. Acceptance of the partial, the temporary, or the just sufficient is often unacceptable for persons with BPD. Unrealistic standards are often maintained in spite of the huge sacrifices that this life-stance demands of them. Most of the initial therapeutic effort with persons with BPD must be spent simply dispelling their sense of hidden shame so that an opening for further communication is possible. The costs exacted by BPD make retrospective analysis extremely painful for them so it is often better to simply deal with the present crisis rather than seeking lasting insight, at least at the beginning of therapy. Life skills should be future oriented and goal directed. The past will only make sense when a firm base is established in present functioning.

This is the primary virtue of behaviorist therapies. By focusing on the present tasks of improving the general environment in which the BPD patient lives boredom and emptiness may be supplanted by a sense of anticipation and reward. Rather than pursuing a steady-state of oblivion and running away from pain or alternatively seeking to internalize pain by adopting it as a form of self-definition the patient with BPD can recover a sense of time experienced as opportunity. Human life is naturally oriented towards the future. The static misery that so often characterizes the borderline existence can be replaced by a gentle gradient of improvement and a balanced appreciation of the joys that accompany everyday experience and that sustain us all on our collective journey of life. Terminal uniqueness is replaced by an acceptance into the general stream of daily functioning without sacrificing their individual identity and personality integrity. Borderlines all too often assume that to join the human race is to be dissolved in the mass. As they learn that the world is an essential part of identity formation and that it is only in encountering tension and opposition that we prevent inner vertigo and orient ourselves, their symptoms will gradually be supplanted by an enduring and mirrored sense of self and personal dignity.

Chapter Seven

Levy-Building Before Landfall

The purpose of this chapter is to address the needs of the caretakers or family members of those who manifest symptoms of BPD. If even seasoned therapists find dealing with persons with BPD to be personally stressful and to require strict procedural safeguards to be in place in order to effectively treat them, it may be imagined how overwhelming close contacts over time may be for those with even a greater investment and care for persons with BPD. It is precisely when these often well-intentioned others overestimate their own abilities that persons with BPD may be abandoned. This disease can in this way claim widening circles of victims. It is not to impute fault to persons with BPD to describe their effect upon others as often manifesting a malign influence.

The phenomenon that psychologists call counter-transference is also experienced in non-professional contacts with persons who manifest BPD. Borderline individuals appeal to our desire to rescue them. They challenge our sense of ourselves as well intentioned people and try our inner resources in various ways.

A sense of the limitation present in all definitions is a handy rule of thumb to go by. The techniques of mapping triggers and specificity of terms have been discussed and I would like now to move on to a further analogy – how to deal with breakdowns in communication with borderline individuals when they occur. The polar extremities of evaluation and expectation that characterize persons with BPD often have an origin in profound inner experiences of prior dislocations and betrayals. The inner coldness and fragmentation that they experience is as real as any of the more commonly shared human experiences simply because these are perceived by persons with BPD with great clarity and intensity.

All human beings are divided from each other by a great abyss. No USB terminal exists to make identical communication possible between our separate souls. We understand each other only through metaphor and sympathy. Only the artists among us can translate inner experience between minds more or less directly because of their unique gifts. The poet Gerard Manley Hopkins hints at the states of mind that borderline persons frequently inhabit. No doubt in past ages it was to literature that people with what today we would call BPD turned for insight into their unique experiences of mood lability and glacial isolation.

Before BPD was ever named as a diagnosable mental illness it must have existed. Such people were no doubt simply viewed as "strange," "difficult," or "trying on the nerves of others." The dark scenario presented by the lives of those who suffer from BPD and the tragic spectacle of waste and poor choices that are manifest in their lives at times resembles something beyond mere human error and appears instead as a manifestation of an alien outside force. It seems impossible that one person could contain such diametrically opposed dispositions.

Love and clarity are superseded by regular bouts of cruel devaluation, paranoid accusations, or vicious fits of jealousy and mistrust often accompanied by other manifestations of a meltdown and dissolution of the self that threatens to drive away those persons and support structures that once lost may not soon be regained. Spirals of alternating alienation and reunion with others become so repetitive that all parties begin to suffer from a variety of post-traumatic stress. Pain itself becomes the binding force between mutual hostages who share a toxic bond from which neither can escape. Outside parties see the ruination that this nameless process claims of its victims and cannot understand the source of the forces that seem to be at play in the relationship. The prospects of dissolution and abandonment, however liberating this occurrence might be for both parties, are insupportable; neither party to the relationship can entertain them. Bound together with bands of steel Borderlines and those who love them descend into an abyss of human misery.

The demanding qualities of the Borderline are the consequence of years of systemic disappointment and frustration as their legitimate needs have not been met. It is as though a point has been reached where revolution supplants reform efforts. The all-or-nothing position of BPD is the result of reaching this point of sustained desperation. Persons with BPD are always seeking out a form of what might be called pseudo-redemption. There is an underlying belief that some person, place, or thing can remove the many anxieties and obsessions that characterize their daily lives. Most of the frustration that borderline patients experience comes from a conviction that this "life-transfusion," this celestial elixir, this magic bullet that will solve all of their problems is being withheld by others for no reason other than to cause the Borderline to suffer deprivation and despair. The constant search for some universal solution to the problems inherent in dealing with a recalcitrant and imperfect world consumes them and makes them rage, even at those who try and help them.

Borderlines can oscillate between opposing positions with remarkable speed, alternating between love and hate, hope and despair, gratefulness and vicious condemnation of others and of themselves. This tragic phantasmagoria provokes bewilderment and chagrin in caretakers and friends. To simply call this cycle one of emotional lability is like calling a hurricane a mere atmospheric disturbance. The sense of unreality that follows the periods of unrelieved stress that one is exposed to in dealing with a person with BPD is akin to the reaction of people who have witnessed terrible accidents or experienced a close-call that might have entailed severe bodily injury. Over many years the result is to produce in other people a combination of skepticism and mistrust of anything that the borderline patient may manifest because virtually everything is a crisis with them. Borderlines feel ignored and abandoned because repeated efforts to tunnel in to their unique region of experience seems hopeless against the resistances that they impose. Finally most other people give up and attempt to move on with their lives.

In an earlier storm analogy I explained that if at sea with a hurricane the prudent choice is to steer clear or risk destruction. Without the protections that can be provided by an in-place and enforceable contract of some sort any dealings with a person displaying BPD symptoms is fraught with emotional risks for all involved. Life is preferably lived in the expectation of prospects of anticipated delight; this hope is what keeps us all going. Hopeful people tend to assume that a life dedicated to misery and destruction is unsustainable and as a result the Borderline is bound to come around if one just hangs in there and endures the various forms of ingenious abuse that are meted out to others by the person with BPD. The sad truth is that by remaining in what I have called the Borderline Situation all that is really being contributed is one other occasion or opportunity for the borderline person to abuse and to destroy whatever relationship has endured the past series of attacks, accusations, or rejections.

Picture the scene after a tornado has passed; witness the waste and devastation, the disorder and the chaos left behind. This is what the history of the borderline life resembles: wreckage, lost opportunities, endless apologies that lure one in for more abuse, confusion and mental pain, and regret on all sides. The coping mechanisms of others are strained to the breaking point by the endless scenes and recriminations that they encounter. Structural flaws of personality that under most circumstances would remain hidden are sliced open and dissected by the compulsion of the Borderline to find evidences of character flaws in others that will match their own level of self-contempt. Borderline persons seem to crave disappointment. The Borderline lives in a merciless world dominated by punishment and pain. Every sign of resurrection is belied by a new crucifixion. There seems to be a perverse triumph in all of this as though the Borderline covets disillusion and failure to support her relentlessly negative view of life and of human beings. It is here that the dark and demonic resemblances to the Borderline's world come into play. Borderlines take up an adversarial stance to everything as though they have been appointed the prosecuting attorney for the world. The only payoff seems to be when the Borderline can finally say, "See, I was right all along; you don't love me."

Tests follow tests but the tasks of reassurance never end. The incline always increases until everything not nailed down begins to slide and objects begin to fall and shatter on the floor of circumstance. Those who care the most tend to re-double their efforts to try and find explanations when the truth is that there are none that will ever be adequate. The aim of the entire enterprise one finally comes to realize has always been to produce defeat and to spread the debris of sorrow and regret as far as the horizon will allow.

This is why BPD is like the tornadoes that precede and accompany the hurricane. A Borderline can maintain multiple or serial dramas simultaneously whereas even one will tend to exhaust most people. In this casino of high-stakes emotional play the Borderline is in the class of the high-rollers. It would help if there was a helpful casino employee at the door to size patrons up prior to admission to the world of the Borderline. There should be a complete evaluation of emotional resources, self-esteem, and lots and lots of leisure time because any and all personal resources will be drawn down towards a zero balance by the relentless attacks and demands of the borderline person. However flush with chips one is when one begins the play the odds are that the evening will end with trips to the credit machine and that one will leave the flashing and well-lit casino with trembling hands, a sour taste in the mouth from stale gin and cigarettes, and walk away alone finally to the parking lot to drive away. The Borderline Casino Bank will have raked in more chips to deposit in the bank account of whatever grim satisfaction the Borderline gets by all of this and by the next night there will be new players because for some reason the piteous plight of the Borderline can be an irresistible draw for people who hope to heal in the Borderline what they should be healing in themselves.

Borderline persons invite a presumption of the power to heal only to reveal that healing was never the point at all. BPD is a disease process that resists every mental antibiotic with the tenacity of a well-entrenched staph infection. The Borderline is determined to keep the pulse-rate of love elevated until cardiac arrest occurs and then to shrug and move along. It isn't abandonment that Borderline's fear as much as it is the transaction costs of finding a new victim. Novelty is nice but there are always those long and boring days and nights until someone new shows up to sign the recruitment papers for a tour of duty on the front lines of emotional Afghanistan. As the situation grows more hopeless there are fewer available recruits and the budget available to be allotted to the war diminish until at last the Borderline may end up making various appeals to unusual quarters for a "coalition of the willing" to assemble for one more try. In the last stages, bereft of all takers and having applied a scorched-earth policy to all the old prospects the Borderline will gather what remains for a final Wagnerian gesture of defiance to a world that did not know the glorious hour of its visitation, all due to this unaccountable need to blight, to weaken, and to destroy.

This is the all-too-common course of BPD. But once the disease is unmasked it is possible to imagine a different outcome. After all a Borderline is a Borderline only as long as he or she plays the game, a game where everyone loses, at the Borderline Casino. A Borderline minus the symptoms that define its course is often a precious and sensitive soul well worth saving. Though time alone can heal, the costs of getting there are far too heavy. For this reason I have written this book to try to unmask a phenomenon that has puzzled many and caused too much pain to all involved.

Contracts with the BPD patient are designed to anticipate risks and to spread costs to those who are able and willing to bear them in hope for greater benefits to accrue at a later date. This is the essence of bargained-for-exchange. Human beings for the most part desire value enhancement, growth, and win-win situations. If BPD is the quintessential case of human waste, then it has seemed to me a classical case for the application of different principles, perhaps even if drawn from the realm of jurisprudence rather than from traditional approaches to insight-therapy.

BPD is in many ways a disease of both cognition and of the will, a rebellion against inherent human limitations. To provide a structural framework, a flying buttress to support the tottering gothic cathedral of the healthy self-perception of the person with BPD rather than the proud and arrogant stance that she may often assume to cover shame has seemed to me to be a valuable addition to the literature on BPD. This structural framework is built by a series of small victories that can provide a template for other small victories. Eventually the dark citadel of BPD symptoms will fall through the gradual inroads made by healthy experiences. The past cannot be erased but it can be resisted by a levy system to protect all parties from the raging waters of this illness until they recede at last and the sunlight returns.

Situations such as those flowing from BPD alter just as any pattern does, element by element. Even tiny changes can break up the fractal pattern of repetitive poor choices and reinforced isolation in the toils and tangles of the life of a patient manifesting the characteristics of BPD. Any gains are to be cherished, celebrated, and used as a new platform from which to advance against the illness. In this way a crisis is always a chance for a turn for the better in what was formerly persistent, resistant, and seemingly invulnerable and entrenched against all efforts of the person with BPD to break free of its coils.

As for therapists and other interested parties in the throes of discouragement my best words to offer you are: strategic retreat to regroup is not to abandon the effort to give aid. In times of trouble it is often good to recall that love endures all things while also recalling that global healing in some cases is only achieved by prayer and fasting.

It is also necessary to realize that some persons with BPD will finally resort to suicide. These losses are never acceptable. It is an article of human faith that no one is a mere adjunct to creation. We are all bound by collective ties that resist this decision to take up armed conflict against one's own life. No matter how great the pain of existing may be, we are not asked to bear with it alone. This life's demands may not be confined to the present order. We little know to what we fly when we seek to break this final synapse that unites us in human community. The totality of a life cannot be encompassed in a single hour nor should it be terminated by a single act. The damage left behind affects many others. The fabric that unites us is forever ripped and altered by such an act. To heal BPD is not easy but we must try to address the despair that can eventuate in such a choice. Even after death these absent ones remain alive to us but in the province of what God alone may now provide for them because they have perished and are beyond what human remedies can provide.

Chapter Eight

Taking to the Lifeboats

As we come closer to the end of this brief book I would like to explore again what we encounter when we deal with this illness either as a patient, as a concerned spectator, or as a therapist. What is primarily involved in BPD is the relentless pursuit of a maladaptive life strategy that has been practiced over many years and honed to a razor's edge. Borderlines presume that their own chaotically shifting perceptions are the way that the world actually is. Tragedy is both normal and normative with them. What this means is that people with BPD assume that others who seem better able to navigate their way through life's situations must be in possession of some strange talismanic power or that they can only manage due to a level of mendacity and duplicity that the Borderline individual scorns to adopt.

People with BPD tend to harbor a global suspicion of the motives of other people combined with an intense envy of their seemingly miraculous ability to transcend the agony that Borderlines face every day of their lives. Those who suffer from BPD feel fundamentally flawed and at times shameful and unclean as though they are infected with some sort of moral leprosy that not only renders them different but culpably so. This despairing inner self-evaluation alternates with its polar opposite, an almost manic sense of entitlement and of special powers that can approach delusional dimensions at times. The point of union, the crossroads of these two contrasting visions of the self is that of the lost child that exists somewhere between them.

Many persons with BPD have yet to successfully navigate the tangle of object-relations that is normally resolved during the separation/individuation stage of child development that usually occurs during the second and third years of life. Borderlines are often said to be lacking in "object constancy." What this means is that when someone is not present he or she is not retained as a nurturing and constant inner object but rather as one that might through being absent begin to dissolve under the assault of the various fantasies or fears that beset the consciousness of the borderline individual. When not actually present to correct the impressions and projections of the Borderline by repeated defenses, assertions, confirmations, or other proofs of devotion that they are willing to live by commitments made and to preserve a basic being-in-relation to the Borderline, a sense of doubt and terror begins to gnaw at the Borderline's confidence and sense of self. Fear arises that other persons have ceased to exist as stable entities that may be trusted; the goodness that was once present might now be morphing into its precise opposite through the same process that seems to force Borderlines into their own shifting ego-states.

This means that part of relating to a borderline person is the necessity of recovering ground that has been lost since the last meeting. The Borderline needs to feel assured that in the interim no decisive change has occurred – that having loved her you do not now inexplicably hate her instead. Even then though there will still be room for nagging doubts. For this reason Borderlines often engage in a sequence of constant testing of the affections of other people. Various obstacle courses are prepared that push others away as a prelude to the inevitable abandonment that the Borderline fears. It is this cycle of inconsistent behavior that tends to undermine the stability of those who have managed to achieve a consistent sense of object-relations for themselves. After an extended time of relating with a Borderline it is common to begin to resemble them in their perennial doubts that they reside in a stable world, one that is worthy of some measure of existential trust.

Even experienced psycho-therapists are subject to this vast undermining of their professional self-esteem when treating borderline patients. Part of the armory of BPD is the ability to possess and use a refined skill (one that is often used on the self) to sense out weak points in the ego-armor and personal defenses of other people. When rage and a sense of inner justification provide the energy an attack by a Borderline can be sudden, global, pervasive, and unrelenting. To oppose that storm is to forget that it is motivated by inner panic and a fear that others will retaliate if a single strand of mental fiber is left intact after the blast.

Borderlines live in an all-or-nothing universe; the stakes are always life and death. Most people tend to find balancing on a tightrope over an existential abyss to be intolerably stressful and anxiety-provoking while to the borderline individual this is simply what life is like in the perceived jungle of human existence. Besides, pain can become secretly exciting and when compared to the emptiness and boredom that appears to the borderline individual to be the only other alternative to living on the edge, pain often seems preferable and even to be empowering. The strain of this mode of living can eventually become intolerable to even the most devoted of friends and family members. The gradual wearing down of affection and understanding can be relentless. Disappointment follows short periods of glimpsed peace and harmony like the prospect of a valley bathed in sunshine and in shade transformed into a desert by the brutal rock faces of vast granite peaks. Should a breakdown or severance finally occur it only serves to confirm the Borderline in the assumption that no one will ever stay the course, that abandonment and betrayal were always the secret agenda of other people, and that the world is one of cosmic and inevitable loneliness and loss. Imagine a mode of coping with life without any stable base in identity of the self or reasonable expectation of constancy in others and you will understand BPD. All of the dimensions of life must be re-negotiated on a daily basis. Like Sisyphus with his rock, life with a Borderline is always lived de novo. It all begins again.

This means that the Borderline situation is always charged with tension. Past successes have little carry-over effect. At the same time past failures need not dictate the failure of hope for a better future for the Borderline. Any therapy decision must be based on the concept of hope. Otherwise the Borderline would simply be consigned to bear his or her burdens alone. Beneath all appearances there exists a desire for wholeness and love in all people and upon this faith all hope of justice and of therapy rest. Negotiation for mutual benefit proceeds on communicated needs and desires. Without communication the human enterprise would long since have failed. Our complex brains demand stimulation, confirmation, and society in the embrace of the human race. But true empathy demands imagination. To bridge alienation perhaps is a definition of the task of human lives.

It is not good therefore to anticipate failure but it is good to recall that all persons by virtue of being human may be tried beyond what endurance can support. Humility alone can sustain us. This is good to help us restore our balance when we deal with BPD. Only those who have had a relationship with a person with BPD can imagine the stress that is involved in the Borderline Situation. As years pass spent in the immediate proximity of a person with BPD one learns what it is to inhabit a private world where the normal rules of life are suspended and replaced by a world of anger, jealousy, and control.

Imagine a solar system with dry planets that once sustained life orbiting about a desolate sun, one lost in the vast abysses of space. The planets exist with only one function to sustain their relationship to the sun. But this sun is a capricious one. At times it will shine with love and radiance and the cold surface of the planets will know something like the glory of dawn, but then a shadow will pass over the surface like a dark hand before weeping eyes and the light will be dimmed or solar flares will reach out like clawing hands begging for help. The space is always too great however for true meeting to occur. Instead there is only a distant reverberation that shakes the surface and sets petrified foliage adrift on the beds of long dead seas; whirlwinds of salt, left by the tears of yesterday, blow out into the desert alone. The damage done inside is the fruit of increasing isolation and of repeated disappointments. Nerves turned like steel piano wires to a point just short of breaking vibrate to the slightest change of tone in a conversation. No degree of watchfulness may be adequate to keep disaster reliably at bay. The shadow of accidents or suicide make every day an open question. Everything most delicate and precious is finally racked and left to rust in the winter rains. Hope is the cruelest thing just as T.S. Eliot once said that April is the cruelest month. It is when happiness and peace seem just within our grasp only to be jerked away to the sound of mirthless laughter that true despair is near. It is then that it is most tempting to follow the advice of many books and of support groups and to leave the person with BPD. But when withdrawal is attempted it is then that the sun will glow one last time and the prospect that it might be self-extinguished is so dreadful that merely to contemplate the possibility is horrible for by now the planet and the sun are as one.

This would be bad enough but one final twist of the screw remains for the sun is actually not a sun at all but a comet that is always swiftly plunging away into endless night and the planet finally realizes that the illusion of orbit has never been true; instead the planets are really more like desolate asteroids each in search of a sun. Where there is BPD there is also the human wreckage of those who participate in the system that sustains the borderline person. This is to know the alternative universe where all who persist in the borderline alternative universe dwell.

Why then enter a contract with someone who is often incapable of abiding by promises? My answer is a simple one, because it is worth a try for all concerned. There is an implied social gradient in dealing with mental illness that anyone who escapes a definition in the various editions of the DSM is functional, mature, and even morally solid. BPD in contrast appears to represent the antithesis of good qualities by virtue of being a sort of bucket diagnosis of unsavory traits all lumped together. Is this not an example of our own discomfort when we see in them what we have long ago silenced in ourselves? Borderline persons are said to manifest any or all of the following characteristics.

These may reflect our exasperation rather than being strictly and uniformly true.

Persons with BPD are said to be:

Unreliable and incapable of keeping commitments

Manipulative and abusive

Confrontational and ill-tempered

Unstable in moods and values

Resistant to efforts to help them

Intolerant of weakness in others

Self-indulgent towards their own faults

Lacking in a stable identity structure

Uncertain of their goals

Subject to sudden enthusiasms that may change frequently

All of which traits might equally be claimed at various times by people who do not qualify for a formal diagnosis of BPD. What this means is that there is a tendency when dealing with the Borderline Situation to engage in a quest for supporting authority to identify "the crazy one" so that at least one party to the relationship can save face and walk away unscathed. It is important to realize that personality variables even when they are dysfunctional do not imply that a person is unworthy of respect or that there may not be profound reasons behind why they act as they do. Any character structure is the product of many choices made over a long period of time, often the best choices that could be made under the person's unique circumstances.

This is important to remember because people with BPD are especially sensitive to criticism that appears lacking in empathy. Dealing with a Borderline is by its very nature intensely confrontational. Ordinary discourse may change tone and quality with astonishing speed. With their razor-sharp perceptions and rigid categories of thought Borderlines can revise valuations of themselves and others with astonishing rapidity. Evaluations that seek a middle-ground or suspended judgment are not usually available to them. This accounts for the love/hate dynamic that usually characterizes relationships with a Borderline. Like working for a strict corporation your job is only as secure as your last quarter's quota of goods sold. Like the fraternity in the film "Animal House" you are always under "double secret probation." The quality control measures of a Borderline would be the envy of any company. The blender of life is never set to anything other than liquefy. No lumps are tolerated in a Borderline's psychic bowl of Crème of Wheat. What this means is that any contract with a Borderline will of necessity have two standards of interpretation: one for the conduct of the Borderline and another one for everybody else. The brilliant therapist of yesterday might be reduced to a being called a self-serving quack tomorrow. In such an atmosphere is a "meeting of the minds" as required by contract ever possible?

Yet I propose that a contract model be adopted and that negotiation should replace simply validating whatever position the person with BPD may choose to adopt. The contract model here proposed is based upon the conviction that the unimpeded course of BPD is so costly to all involved that desperate measures are necessary to preserve the life, safety, and sanity of all involved in what I have called the Borderline Situation. To propose limits to people who are accustomed to behaving as if there were none will not be easily accepted. For this reason their world of choices must contract until it can provide an adequate containment vehicle for Borderline aggression. To use an analogy drawn from the Second World War, the place and time to intervene is when the Borderline troops first attempt to occupy the Rhineland rather than to wait for a later blitz attack on Poland. The end goals of the illness once they have been discerned clearly must be opposed with all the forces at our command. BPD is no one's friend. It is an utterly destructive orientation to the world and to others and above all to the patient herself. Its logistics are clear. Like a cancer it must be deprived of the nutrients that sustain its growth. Contract principles can shut down and starve the disease of the nutrients it requires and prevent the pre-conditions from developing into harm to the person with BPD before that harm occurs by prescribing various reductions or new allocations of necessary resources.

I believe that the course of BPD is alterable by resource deprivation, not to the Borderline individual herself, but to the insidious BPD process. This diversion of resources is accomplished by making substitute gratifications available at the same time as those usually proposed by the illness and then inviting a comparison of results over time by the patient herself. This process involves building new habits through imposing temporary duress upon the old habits and depriving them of their paradoxical reinforcing effect. It is the exertion of quiet force like a splint on a broken limb to sustain it while it heals; it is a process analogous to braces applied on the teeth by an orthodontist. This is the method of dealing with the Borderline Situation proposed here. It is only a proposal. Every contract must begin though with an offer awaiting either acceptance or a counter-offer. Costs can only be estimated and assessed in the presence of alternatives. The biggest problem with BPD is that those who suffer from it are either overwhelmed by too many options or by too few. Meaningful freedom of choice lies along the spectrum of what might be called reasonable options and the necessary time for reflection to choose intelligently from among them.

To wait for spontaneous improvement over time by the Borderline is to run great risks, risks that are unnecessary as well as costly. The Borderline's determined habit of thought is to disable and destroy any and all efforts to offer effective aid. The same egocentricity that refuses or at least is unable to sustain productive as opposed to shame-based self-criticism is relentless in its ability to sound out flaws in others as mentioned above. This process has been called "projective-identification." Borderline patients tend to adopt a policy of blame-deflection by attacking others and inducing in them the helplessness and other flaws that they feel to be so characteristic of their own condition. So successful are they at this defense and so single-minded in their pursuit of it that Borderlines seem to succeed in remaining ill at times only through sheer grit and determination.

The rewards, though they are incomprehensible to others, are the same paradoxical inversion of pain and pleasure by which they hope to adjust to a world that they feel will inevitably disappoint them. Add to this a certain craving for punishment for past offenses when they are in a phase of self-denigration and it is clear why Borderlines are so often alternately victims or victimizers.

To draw a line between the person and the illness that she may manifest is not easy. The Borderline Situation is relentlessly destructive to anyone who dares to enter the forbidden zone where the storm is raging. For this reason it is best if all else fails to seek out a life-boat and be ready to board it if the vessel is truly sinking and to reluctantly push away from the side. The reverberations from a person with BPD that is sinking lower and lower in the water can destroy other people as well and it may be best to take one's chances on the open sea rather than to be sucked down in the vortex produced by the sinking vessel. If by chance or blessing the life of the Borderline remains afloat, and some manage to endure against almost insuperable odds, there is always the chance that years later a chance meeting on the street will reveal that time has healed them where everything else has failed. I am not counseling abandonment here but limitation of damages when literally nothing more can be done against a Borderline's willed destruction.

From the beginning BPD has been used as a holding category for individuals whose symptoms and functioning were variable, fluid, and contradictory. The broad BPD diagnosis still seeks to define a set of workable parameters for this illness and to contain and restrain the members of this diverse group of patients as they pursue their destructive life-courses with often unabated vigor in spite of all interventions. There was a time when such persons were simply called difficult or impossible. And it is anyone's guess what names shall be given to them in future issues of the DSM. What is important is that the symptoms broadly or narrowly defined should be addressed.

A simple functional test for BPD might be: if you notice that you are angry, ashamed, dismayed, and compassionate by degrees when dealing with an individual or if your hair is turning prematurely grey when you are not pulling it out of your head when you are with them, then it is probable that you are dealing with a person with BPD. If you have any leverage at all you might consider adopting a contractual approach to restoring some degree of order and solace to your life. If this fails then the final assessment may need to be to reluctantly add your portion to the self-fulfilling prophesy of doom that many Borderlines embrace by gently letting go and moving on. This letting go need not be irrevocable but it is important that the borderline person realize that to court irrevocability and finality with other people is a dangerous game. Even death may be the outcome of BPD by deliberation, impulse, or accident, unnecessary and deplorable as this irrevocable result may be.

I have written this book to point the way upwards to a better life for all involved with BPD. There is no one best and perfect life. The terms of existence are always being re-negotiated against recalcitrant circumstances. What cannot be remedied must be mourned. But then we must move on. Time teaches us to moderate our demands on life. The sages of China define a world of changes and reversals as the only world that we inhabit. By expecting change the melancholy bred of loss and regret is moderated by confidence in the option of seeking a restoration of what has been lost. So while it may not yet be possible to write the Borderline epic it may be possible to pen a few lines on rice paper like a Haiku verse. I have tried to do so here.

There are always favorable occasions that will allow one at times to penetrate the barbed wire, the trenches, and the gun emplacements behind which the Borderline seeks shelter from a hostile world, one where anyone might prove to be a spy or traitor or come armed with bombs like a terrorist. The battle for stability within the psyche of the Borderline is a costly one of addiction, self-cutting, tearful or irate accusations, of regrets, and later apologies that may prevent present abandonment but only to prolong the varied cycle of abuse. But there are moments when negotiations of some sort may proceed and a contract of sorts may be reached.

To expect strict performance is usually an illusory hope, but progress in identifying and naming issues and trigger points for BPD acting-out may still be made. Familiarity may gradually accustom the Borderline to realize that she is in fact coping better for various lengths of time and that she is managing to make short gliding flights before coming to earth again. By linking chains of accomplishment and pointing out patterns of relative success it may be possible over time for the Borderline to reach a point of trust in experience around which a stable self can coalesce. This is the beginning of healing.

In this life we aid each other to endure and at times we even triumph over seemingly insuperable odds. It is this that can substitute hope for disillusionment and awaken faith again in the human enterprise. It is one that will always remain a struggle with a contingent world: one that is subject to chance, to choice, and to the results of both once events have occurred and been enshrined in time's irrevocable scroll. Learning to live successfully in the world is to accept the inevitable gap between what we can foresee and control and what materializes unforeseen out of the matrix of events. It is here that those who suffer with BPD merge with the ordinary strategies that we all must use to deal with life's inevitable joys and sorrows, our triumphs and our mistakes. To ask for more is to posit a different world, one in which negotiation would be unnecessary and no illnesses such as BPD would exist to be diagnosed and treated with all the forces at our command.

Chapter Nine

The Psychology of BPD

A book such as this one is of necessity incomplete and impressionistic and this chapter is even more so. The psychology of BPD is far too complex to be reduced to a chapter summary. What this chapter represents then is a personal summation of various items that have struck me as significant in my readings in the psychological literature on this complex subject. As such it represents an appeal to the reader to do likewise. There remains much theoretical conflict regarding the nature of BPD and how it should best be treated. It is bad enough to meet confusion from within the patient herself, but it is even more challenging when therapists disagree among themselves.

Each angle of approach may reveal what has hitherto been hidden from others. Just as case law refines static concepts drawn from what lawyers call "black letter law," so does each case history of someone with BPD enlarge our knowledge by giving it a specific and concrete form in one set of life events. There are many ways that someone can be diagnosed as borderline. The shifting nature of their symptoms over time and under various conditions of stress or its absence further complicates this broad diagnostic category.

The origins and causes of BPD are matters of much debate and many theories as to its nature have been elaborated over time. Most of these theories presume that what is operative in BPD is a fragmentation of the personality into various sub-personalities and partial interior objects that manifest an overall failure to achieve stability in self-object relations. This condition is held to have been of longstanding duration, perhaps traceable as far back as the very first years of life. At that time the infant enters a period of testing limits with her primary caregivers. The successful negotiation of this stage of development is manifested by the emergence of a unique self, one that is not riddled by anxiety that separation will result in losing the security of her former unified relations with significant others.

Negotiating this phase of separation and individuation can be vitiated by inducing separation before the child is ready or by preventing it when she is ready to try her limits. If the infant perceives that attempts at individuation will result in the loss of the nurturing maternal or paternal objects upon whose good-will and aid her survival is based, she may abandon the necessary tasks of individuation, of reaching out into the world as the separation/individuation stage of human development requires. If the infant is held too closely by anxious parental figures, separation may be felt by the infant to threaten the parents' own sense of stability and thus to risk retaliation by their fears or displeasure. Similarly, if she is pushed into separation prematurely rather than based on her own spontaneous wishes, she will fear that to individuate is the equivalent of death and thus seek to retain her former merged object-relations rather than to risk the grievous loss of her caregivers.

This is no effort to assign conscious culpability to a Borderline's primary care-givers for this failure to achieve what has been termed object-constancy in the young child. What is important is to recognize that the present fears entertained by the Borderline individual of object-loss and the identity diffusion of the Borderline are not without a basis in her developmental history. The alternating fear of abandonment combined with angry blame when her fears are activated can be traced back to this failure to differentiate self from other. Borderline individuals have great difficulty in recognizing the independent needs and indeed existence of other people; for the Borderline other people are either perceived as good and thus perceived as literally parts of themselves or they are perceived as bad and engaged in maliciously or selfishly withdrawing the necessary nurturing supplies that keep the Borderline secure in her world and plunging her into a state of abandonment with its attendant feelings of emptiness and desolation. Borderlines tend to fall into patterns of negotiating this problematic and anxiety-ridden dilemma by alternately engulfing other people by controlling or abusive bonding and then switching to swift and angry actions to push people away as having no worth for the temporarily omnipotent borderline personality. It is this swift sequence of desperate need combined with callous disregard that is so confusing to other people and a cause of such dismay to those who really love and care for borderline individuals.

In order to address these symptoms, which cause so much pain to all involved in the Borderline Situation, two main therapeutic approaches are being used at this time. The most common approaches in therapy with persons diagnosed as Borderline are Dialectical-Behavioral Therapy (DBT) and what is called Psychodynamic Therapy which uses the transference dynamics of the analysis to convey insights to the patient with the hope that insight will gradually yield a voluntary control of errant impulses. Both approaches may be considered to use a skill that is analogous to the Buddhist concept of mindfulness. An attitude of mindfulness asks that we suspend action until clarity is obtained as to what is actually occurring. As reflection and delay takes the place of the acting-out of feelings desperately and impulsively BPD patients gain coping skills and a measure of control over the dysfunctional habits manifested by BPD.

It will still be helpful even as recovery progresses to have a structure of support and containment in place to provide an adjunct sense of grounding when partial meltdowns inevitably occur during the course of treatment. Persons with BPD cannot be expected to assume a responsibility overnight that is the fruit of a process of skill acquisition and the breaking of old habits of substitute gratification in dealing with their pain. The general trajectory of "up-and-out," short term therapies should be replaced by a therapy of nurturing that can provide effective support without preventing the essential individuation of the patient to be gradually achieved by her over time.

Borderlines will attempt to engage therapists and those in other relationships with them in the repetition of their primary dilemma by seeking a perfect merger and identification with them and then by raging whenever this proves to be impossible to achieve as it inevitably is by adult persons. A person with BPD does require though extra aid to escape the trap in which she has become enmeshed. For many Borderlines in their present circumstances the very concept of health may be more of an act of faith than a remembrance of things past since a sense of stability has always eluded them. But patience in their regard does not mean suspending ongoing efforts to dislodge them from their current state of pseudo-functioning. Existing with symptoms of BPD present is an inherent no-win situation and the essence of a non-sustainable life position. When this becomes clear to all parties negotiation for change becomes possible and the essential resources can be assembled and effectively deployed for what amounts to a deliverance.

This campaign of deliverance must be a sustained one and partial reverses must be taken in stride. Persistence is required by life itself as lived in time. Just as history does not end but rather must encapsulate losses and continue, so does the course of a human life in this world of ours. It is natural when witnessing someone in distress to want to be of aid and those in the helping professions possess a word for what results when our humanity overcomes our judgment – that word is "counter-transference." Borderlines tend to beckon us beyond the zone of professionalism that exists to safeguard both client and professional during therapy. A balance of interventions may be difficult to achieve. Once out on open ground with BPD there are few guide-posts for mutual expectations or stable roles and effective therapy is often vitiated by events. All parties must feel their way slowly and be prepared to retrace their steps when necessary.

Borderline persons are accustomed to living in a world without a normative compass while most people are not. This may at first seem to indicate an advantage for the Borderline in interactions but in fact what is entailed is that Borderlines invite various forms of exploitation by the unconscious needs that exist in all people. Even therapists find themselves becoming effectively spell-bound by the various ploys and devices by which the Borderline will first strip them of defenses and then play a siren song to lure them on to their destruction. The nature of the appeal is the desire to help, to exercise skills competently, and to emerge with self-esteem intact. By being incorporated into the web of BPD individuals often find themselves engaging in their own projections of affect and resentment toward the Borderline. Since in turn persons with BPD tend to be as suggestible as they are subject to induce suggestions in others a sort of mutual hypnosis of therapist and patient tends to occur. All parties to interactions with a Borderline tend to behave as though scripted toward obtaining some inscrutable and tragic finale. This is why mapping the situation is so essential. It is essential to understand what is actually occurring outside of the distorted world into which one is gradually co-opted by life-events shared with a person with BPD.

Counter-transference was in its origins a Freudian term but its application far exceeds the strict realm of psychoanalysis or other forms of therapy. What is actually entailed is a degree of induced hyper-reactivity over time to the various provocations of borderline behaviors. The deeper the relationship with a person with BPD, the more incapacitated one may become. Worse still the more the Borderline is incapacitated in turn by succeeding in harming other people. This downward spiral must be broken. Borderline patients tend to be so deeply wedded to diminishment and to destruction that they lose with every seeming victory that reinforces their symptoms the little independence and healthy identity that they may possess. The impatience and anger of others towards them only adds to their shame and fears of abandonment while their powerful attacks of rage when they are directed towards other people only serve to add to their contempt and mistrust of other people for enduring it and coming back for more abuse.

The Borderline situation is thus one of multiple losses. Each party seeks to prevail and to dominate the other, no meeting of the minds occurs, and no mutual benefit is achieved through the exchanges and interactions. Absent agreement what is achieved instead is a constant state of jockeying for position in a race to nowhere. Even after years of therapy many Borderlines and their therapists must regretfully and often resentfully admit that little real progress has been made. There is none of the partial closure that is entailed in real progress – healing still remains in prospect. The therapy is revealed as always having been about a power-struggle after all. By winning the battle in not getting well the person with BPD really loses in the larger arena of her life.

The use of power over another person rather than seeking mutual benefits tends to be inherently self-defeating. Consent can never be productively coerced because to do so leads to the generation of various externalities – what is gained must be paid for later at a more inconvenient time and often with greater overall effort expended than if a compromise had been reached earlier. This is a truth that nations might well recall as they strive for the intimidation provided by various systems of weaponry. To admit defeat is a bitter thing, yet it is often the only pathway to real bargaining for a mutual exchange of benefits. What we are owed through debt or fear cannot be freely given. To seek to compel recovery then is often to ensure that the disease of BPD will persist. At some point the person who manifests the symptoms of BPD must take it to heart that though a certain degree of what might be called life-force transfusion may occur between people there is a zone of inevitable loneliness that surrounds us all so that human freedom is even possible. Taking responsibility means negotiating for what we need or desire.

The person with BPD is responsible to seek out the means of her own healing. No matter how much one may desire to save a sufferer from BPD it is essential to recall that for a borderline patient, whose very depths may have been so infused by various unfortunate life-events that their very concept of self can be at stake, to be rid of their pain by main force exerted by fiat is an act of disrespect and a futile enterprise with no real prospect of success. Instead, their life experience must be honored in all of its chaos and contradiction, not because it is functional or desirable, but simply because it is what they experience. What from the outside may appear to be a string of unnecessary tragedies may from within the borderline patient herself appear to have been all along the force of an ineluctable destiny. When we respect the Borderline patient enough to admit that we are powerless to compel change or to mandate that she see the world differently than in fact she does see it, then it may be possible for her to adopt that stance or position from which all recovery must begin – to suspend her judgment long enough to effectively contemplate change.

It is this phenomenon of soul-healing that was made manifest in the famous story from the gospels where a woman caught in adultery was brought before Jesus. As the men who had accused her drifted away a point came where only Jesus and the woman were left. Jesus asked her if anyone had condemned her. She answered that no one had. Jesus answered, "Neither do I condemn you." He sends her on her way to live a better life. To suspend judgment in human affairs is not to approve but to realize that condemnation of other people works no real good. Only from the point of view of love is hatred perceived in its inherent malice. Only in wholeness do we realize how inadequate a formerly fragmented perspective really was.

The best of the therapeutic approaches for BPD advise adopting this position of objective bracketing and delay rather than acting upon impulses or in panic. We all exist in the suspense of the moment and decisions made are often vastly premature. To do nothing is usually best when any action taken will only serve to augment the confusion and pain. Refection allows time for deliberation and from deliberation exercised consistently over time comes wisdom, virtue and that integrity that Borderlines and all of us find so elusive and difficult to achieve in our lives.

The business of living is painful and perilous for one who must contend with BPD. The fragmentation of various borderline states makes daily functioning difficult for them in ways that most people cannot imagine. Small setbacks can assume the magnitude of major disasters and easily overwhelm the Borderline's immediate coping capabilities. Add to this a general suspiciousness of the motives of others and an expectation of immanent betrayal or abandonment and it will be readily seen how confusing and imperiled everyday life is for those who suffer from BPD. Their everyday world can appear as an empty desert; it may manifest the glacial frigidity and sinister undercurrents reminiscent of the works of Franz Kafka. Between the polarities of boredom and panic the Borderline is often caught like a deer in the headlights of a speeding car. Their appearance and manner to others may vary from that of a forlorn waif to that of a demanding autocrat.

For the person with BPD this is not experienced as character contradiction but rather as the appropriate responses to outer stimuli and inner states. Borderlines feel always on the defensive against what they assume are the naturally superior coping mechanisms of other people. The Borderline's own shifting and precarious life-stance implies that the universe should be on-call to meet her urgent needs. Reckless and self-destructive behaviors are the unfortunate result of desperate efforts to re-attain a sense of control and solace. She may feel that if she did not exercise constant vigilance and effort she would cease to exist. It takes a constant input of data, excitement, and stimulation to prevent her sense of self from being compromised by various sources of doubt, shame, or anxiety. Each waking hour is problematic because the contents are not directly willed or controllable. Living on the edge seems to bestow a heightened sense of self, one that seems to give an electric charge to her existence that will not be bled off as soon as the outside stimuli cease. Emptiness and self-reproach are always there to resume their hegemony of gnawing pain in the borderline consciousness.

Much of the acting out and impulsiveness of BPD patients is due to this sense of frenzy and desperation as the Borderline patient labors to avoid what psychiatrists used to call decomposition into unstable or psychotic ego-states. Much of this terror can be prevented by having a support structure in place and ready to guide her actions when things become simply overwhelming for her. This structure combined with a gradually acquired ability to seek an inner calm within before taking immediate and what are often ill-considered actions, those that only make the situation worse, will be of inestimable benefit to her. Day-to-day existence can also be improved for the Borderline patient by having multiple emergency support strategies ready-to-hand until her feelings stabilize after temporary sources of stress pass. When she is better able to return again to a degree of life-management, she may discard sources of temporary outside succor. In times of comparative calm it is possible to point out common factors in her behavior and general themes in her past relationships; insight of the result of repetition.

It is also possible to make life easier for Borderline patients by treating their chronic distress with anti-depressants and dealing with periods of acute crisis with anti-anxiety medications. But the overall goal must always be to reconcile the borderline patient with the contingent nature of human existence and to teach her the necessary coping skills so that she can attain full functioning in a world that demands maturity, self-reliance, and the sacrifice of immediate solace for the attainment of longer-term goals.

The conflict between expectations and reality are not characteristic of BPD alone; they are part of the universal human condition. One of the reasons that BPD remained without recognition for so long and even at the present time implicates many other co-occurring diagnoses is that the BPD population includes many individuals with remarkable sensitivity to the stresses and confusions of life in the post-modern world. The demands made upon all of us in a rapidly changing and globalized world tend to atomize and isolate the individual. Our identities tend to become constructions that are assembled ad hoc to meet the expectations and requirements of the various roles we must play in the various networks of association that we access. It is all like one continuous interview and the final resume of who we consider ourselves to actually be has finally been revised so many times that it becomes a mere fictional composition. Everything becomes a gesture awaiting an answering response. Borderline persons may simply be those who find these daily adaptations to a moving set of platforms to be too demanding and meretricious to justify the effort.

Yet the human need for reflection and connection is a constant. Caught between human needs that are universal and the swift vernacular of conflicting voices that surround them, borderline persons tend to take various entrenched positions of defense and end up fighting the world and blaming themselves or others in alternation when their desperate life-tactics do not work. The circular descent into chaos of those with BPD might in other ages have been circumvented by more minimal expectations in social conditions. Fewer life-options were offered then, particularly to women. If BPD is a diagnosis most often met with in the female population and if lack of a stable identity and emotional lability are its primary indicators, then it may be that social factors are as much in play as innate psychological causes for BPD. This view is further supported by the age of onset of BPD in the late teens and early twenties when expectations and aspirations are at their height for young people from both outside and inside the individual. It is only after negotiating many life crises that the resilience of maturity is attained. BPD symptoms tend to lessen over time as life-skills increase and an attitude of toleration replaces rage when inevitable obstacles are met. As demands decrease actual rewards tend to increase because we learn over time to demand less from life than unconditional surrender to our wills from recalcitrant circumstances. Dogged resistance is replaced by willingness to compromise to attain our immediate goals and to wait for whatever remains in patience.

Lawyers learn in the course of their training that clarity is seldom perfectly obtainable in the law. The goal of law is always a quest for the possible rather than the ideal. The art of compromise and openness to the settlement of conflicting claims shares much in common with the techniques of Dialectical-Behavioral Therapy (DBT). When a diagnosis of BPD is seen as an opportunity for negotiation to begin rather than for a simple quick-cure the prognosis for people with BPD improves significantly. The approach of this book has been to allow each person with BPD to identify her areas of special sensitivity, each with certain predictable triggers that tend towards maladaptive responses. Change can occur when reactions are thwarted by pre-planning ways to break the causal chain between stimulus and response.

Quarrels are too often seen by borderline patients as signs of rejection by other people demanding a breaking away from the relationship and demonization of the person, place, or thing that was formerly needed, valued, and loved. Disagreements need not be final. The weakness of all superlatives (best, most, eternal) is that even one case of exception disproves the rule. People with BPD can learn that most generalizations in life are governed more by probability than by the certainty of strict accounting methods. The desperate search for the ultimate all too often denies them the enjoyment of the possible and the adequate. Needs are never met once and for all in human life. The words "happily ever after" are usually a sign that the author has run out of ideas for his story.

Just as life is without perfect satisfaction in most respects and will always provide a measure of resistance to our efforts to get our needs and wants met, so it is also without the neat closure provided by a movie, novel, or romance. The aesthetic norms applicable to works of art are supplied by the author and are a function of the genius of literary production to suggest themes that can on occasion be met with in life. The fact that so many of the plays of Shakespeare end with bodies littering the stage as the various actions reach their tragic consequences shows how often human endeavors are met with resistance and how often chance determines outcomes rather than human ingenuity. As the energy of the play is spent the audience is sent forth chastened and made wise by what they have just witnessed. Aristotle termed this the purging function of art, which by evoking pity and terror reminds us of our human limitations and teaches us a moral lesson - to seek contentment where alone it can be found in humility and in graceful resignation to fate.

Even in Shakespeare however there are characters that in spite of age still persist in a desire to exercise supreme control over life and are ready to seek to impose their will on all that surrounds them. A little time reading King Lear is advisable for all retired persons before writing their wills and some time reading Romeo and Juliette may chasten the presumption of youth that the quickened pulses of love are the equivalent of having found a premature heaven in an equally benighted adolescent's ardor. Humor is the saving grace of humankind and blessed are they who discover early its benefits in keeping us all sane. Pity is seldom of use except when felt for another person's pain; when applied to ourselves it may swiftly yield bitterness rather than the momentary expression and release for which tears were designed.

Some of the wisest words ever uttered were to let the dead bury their dead. What is past must be followed by new things. Nothing on earth is permanent and even the planet may dip on its axis from time to time for all we know. The search for order is precisely that, a search. The adaptability of women to the demands of life and the organic impositions of female existence is a virtue too often neglected in the annals of the heroic. The astonishing thing is that in the face of all the wars, epidemics, and famines that have beset the human race, the human species has yet thrived and now covers the earth. The healing capacity of the individual and of the species is such as to both astonish us and to admonish us when despair seems near.

By viewing life in its correct proportion to eternity we are comforted. The present is always suspended over the abyss of history and always dwarfed by the vast potentialities of the unknown sea of the future. To rest comfortably upon the surging billows of the present is to rise and fall as the waves pass beneath us leaving the unresisting craft of our lives unharmed. Just as a boat must negotiate wind, wave, and current so must each life sail its unique course and find harbor when the voyage is done. As individualism has come to take the place of family, tribe, and nation as the center of emphasis we have come to demand too much of each other and to abstract too far from the context of events. By resisting all assimilation into higher orders and collectives we each think to become the sole arbiters of truth.

When all things become subjective though, true subjectivity is lost. The subjective is always seeking relation to what is objective and not created from within us. Men and women are not gods. Our status as creatures provides the blessed limits that sustain us.

It may be that BPD is a sort of metaphysical disease caused by a premature desire to possess eternity in an imperfect world. Its characteristics of alternate overweening pride and desolation are the result of the internalizing of unrealistic norms because of the unmet needs or abuse encountered in the childhoods of those who suffer from it. Shame, guilt, abuse, violence, or abandonment: all of these and more can yield the personality deficits or distortions that may take on the clinical form of BPD. The healthy course of human development will always be the one that recognizes the great constants of human nature. Human beings are born with the expectation of a sane social order and a need for love and relatedness.

It is the task of the leaders among us to try and provide the superstructure that makes sane and healthy individual development possible. The strength of the center is known by the condition of all who exist on the periphery of life, those on the borderlines of human functioning. By negotiating with the borderlines of life and of the human condition in all respects we in fact are negotiating with ourselves to adopt a course on a stormy sea, one with some prospect for safety and salvation at last. We all might prefer to live in a world without risk or consequences. Much of the thinking and work of the law is dedicated to assessing and allocating risks of loss and in devising remedial measures when losses occur. The real-world approach to BPD taken in this book is similar to the tasks that lawyers must face each day as they encounter the resistance of statutes and the precedents found in case law and seek to find a way to weave fact and law together in a way that benefits their clients.

BPD is a disorder of rigid and maladaptive stances undertaken to address a changing world. The symptoms of BPD are unsustainable over time without engendering great stress for the borderline person and others. Isolation is inadequate as a remedy. A hermit-like life is no solution. A sense of shame and self-contempt often freeze the Borderline in place rather than leading her to liberation. To ask for help when in distress is not a failure. Change requires support during the transition period as the person with BPD tries new approaches and incorporates healthier habits of mind, those that are better adapted to the often impatient and intransigent world in which we all must live. The fragile self must leave its shell behind and be exposed for a time if it is to thrive. Small steps in this direction will develop their own momentum over time. This is the goal of a contractual model for dealing with the daily negotiations imposed by dealing with a person with BPD.

Chapter Ten

Briefing the Case

Although success in dealing with someone with BPD can in no way be presumed it has seemed advisable here to act as an advocate on their behalf and to presume that with labor and good-will much can be achieved. This is appropriate to a book that is more of a reflection upon a phenomenon than it is a manual of therapy or a how-to-book. There is no easy principle of verifiability when dealing with something that may change form hour by hour and day by day. The mystery and the mystique of every individual are largely unfathomable.

The very existence of BPD testifies to the individuality of the human condition and its variability over time. The basic tonality of our lives may vary from the major to the minor keys. It is difficult to explain to people who have always known love, security, and a generally welcoming attitude from other people what it is like for people that share life experiences that have been ones of betrayal, sudden alterations in relationships or living standards, or perhaps of physical and mental abuse. There may even be an inborn disposition towards irritability of the senses that makes borderline persons less tolerant of the variable conditions that life's events impose upon them. To witness the swift alterations in their perceptions and responses can be quite alarming and may account for the wary distance that many people may adopt in dealing with someone with BPD.

This swiftness and extremity of response may not be unique to them however. The very conditions that can produce artistic ability or genius may result in psychic instability as the lives of many writers and artists demonstrate. Why do so few members of the human race leave a record of their perceptions in music, paintings, or novels? What drives them to seek through their unique medium to translate their private worlds and visions that though in many ways unique still manage to awaken an answering response somewhere from deep within ourselves?

There is an abiding climate of the soul and a private language that each of us speaks from within ourselves, that realm that none shall ever penetrate because it is ours alone. We navigate about each other like fast sailing craft in a narrow bay each pursuing his or her separate course, reluctant to tack or come about to yield the seaway to another.

To find general love is rare and we do well to obtain mere gentility from others and few are the people of whom we can claim that they truly understand us. Fame is the province of the few. Even then the scrutiny that we visit upon the private lives of celebrities is intended to discover their faults in most cases rather than to understand and to sympathize with the burdens of their notoriety. We often imagine them to be happier than they are.

The vast collectives that dominate our lives care little for the fate of the individual. Even the social media sites that allow us access to the global networks of discourse by the sheer numbers linked together can reduce us to just one more set of data posted on the web. Can there ever really be a global village? Are not the pervasive lotteries that claim our spare dollars a sign of our contemporary desperation to be transformed by chance overnight into the modern equivalent of royalty if our number should be picked? Is our real life so insupportable that we take out such long odds on happiness? Isn't daily life diminished by the mere expectation that such an acme of wealth would be supportable by our frail egos?

Think for instance of the many options that cascade down upon the winners of lotteries. Relationships are often imperiled in anticipation of various gifts. New needs surface as the winner looks down from her new Olympian height at the life that only yesterday seemed to offer at least some degree of satisfaction and of pride. We are each condemned to carry about with us a past reservoir of memory. The moving finger writes and the resulting scroll long or short is irrevocable. To edit a life is not possible as it is with a manuscript. There is no command to cut, paste, or delete.

The future however can amend the past by supplanting habits of destruction with healthier ones. We may even be grateful for the limitations imposed by past events because they give significance to our actions now. The present dispensation of our lives cannot tolerate too many options. The best things about us are those things that define our limits. Loyalty and love demand limitation as does our personal integrity. Unfortunately the present state of technology is bestowing upon each of us a volume of choices that can lead to anomie. Experience merges with experience until all becomes one vast undifferentiated whole. Stories demand a beginning, middle, and an end. An encyclopedic life finally becomes meaningless. The computer is not a model of the human mind if we really understand our humanity. There are no leaps of insight in computers, no ecstasy, and no contemplation of the still point around which a life may spool itself. Aspirations to eternal continuity and omnipotence in our present state destroy the balance of the human equation and leave us lost as singularities placed among the multitude of persons and events that are jostling about us like atoms in solution.

The need for limits is not confined to the human personality. The closure that defines a book finally becomes arbitrary if it aspires to be more than it is; more words might always be written. When vast libraries may ride about in one's pocket the value of each word tends to be diminished. Information becomes just so many bytes or pixels displayed on a screen. To burn a book seems an appalling act while to delete a text is the work of an instant. All of the above is meant to raise the question of the value of the personal, the mark that we may leave upon each other by sharing a common human nature while still remaining unique and irreplaceable in ourselves.

When applied to mental illnesses this careless disregard for the unique becomes even more visible. BPD manifests itself in turmoil and a fracturing of experience in pursuit of the unattainable. Emotions slosh about like water in a heavily laden sailing-craft's bilge or an ill-packed load in a moving van. People with BPD ask at once too much and too little from life.

Ours is a world that is often impatient with people who are far less abrasive than those with BPD often are. The intransigent postures that they can take demand that the world adjust to them and it is loath to do so, regarding them all too often as merely noxious and unruly individuals while ignoring their pain, buried as it is beneath so much that appears immature and invasive as they leave the results of their chaotic perceptions and impulsive actions behind them. Meanwhile, those of us who love people with BPD must often pay a heavy price for that very devotion. Unfounded fits of jealousy from the Borderline can incapacitate those whose protestations of fidelity are resisted and discounted. It is as though people with BPD hunger for disappointment and thrive on what they most fear. Pain becomes so much the general milieu of their days and nights that ordinary joy becomes inconceivable. To be for an instant out of their lover's regard poses a threat of eternal separation for them.

The human dilemma of BPD is written large for all to see and in doing so we recognize that in many ways their pain is universal and contemporary as well as individual. Our approach to BPD tells us as much about ourselves as it does about those who suffer from this diagnosis. There has been insufficient study of the relations between mental disorders and the unique politics and history of the age in which the patient and therapist find themselves living. An example is the non-directive therapy of Richard Rogers that appears now to mirror the open searching for insight and enlightenment of the late twentieth century. Similarly the prevalence of hysteria addressed by the early papers of Sigmund Freud was precisely what one would expect to have encountered in the repressed world of the latter 19th century. Even today's emphasis upon behaviorism mirrors the managerial perspective and the neo-pragmatism that attempts to simply get the patient functioning again and productive so that they can rejoin the global race.

The plea of the borderline patient to be understood is best addressed it seems to me by the phenomenological approach of the psychological movements more commonly studied on the continent, Germany and France. Examples are provided by the existential and phenomenological works of Ludwig Binswanger and in the philosophy of Maurice Merleau-Ponty. Only by entering the unique world-view of the borderline patient can those questions be answered that obsess these often very talented and volatile individuals.

Our impatience with the individual mapping of the lived-world of a single person has blinded us to some of the fundamental categories of human experience. The contemporary world is suspicious of any dysfunction for the simple reason that it is compressed, fast-paced, and stressed by events. We are living in a world that is virtually simultaneous. By this I mean that our personalities and expectations of life are the product of events that are occurring "right now in real time. We hold out little hope that strands drawn from such divergent perspectives as those that are presented in a global marketplace of ideas can be successfully woven into a synthesis. We esteem short-term market evaluations and ignore any effort to achieve real insight into the perennial human condition. We often fail to even perceive that certain perennial questions must be answered again and again as each generation grapples with its own unique circumstances.

All of this cannot but add to the distress of borderline patients who are often engaged in seeking the ideal and are often caught between irreducible extremes. Ambiguity and irresolution is their daily experience. Will not such a chaotic outer world fail to produce fruitful results for them? Will not exhaustion ensue from all this leaping about in search of salvation, of perfect love, of ideal friendship, or of idealized personal integrity, that once-and-for-all solution that will finally bring them the perfection, stability, and peace that they so crave? The virtues of most contemporary therapies for BPD are to enable the Borderline to moderate such extreme demands and to tolerate frustrated hopes. The reality of the outer world often denies our most sanguine aspirations. There is a quiet stoicism that lies behind sound behavioral approaches to human volatility. The first imperative is to preserve each human life and to await a better day.

Though I do not mean to criticize behavioral therapeutic approaches here, I do desire to point out that no mental illness is ever entirely counter-productive for the sufferer. Some of the greatest artists and writers have manifested symptoms of what we would call mental illness. Health is more than a mere bland adjustment to things as they are. The human race owes much to its madmen and its cyclonic personalities. A bovine placidity might make for peace but hardly for insight. The complexity of the human brain and our scope of imagination make us prone to what might be termed "emergent visions." Perfect anticipatory control would stifle innovation and creativity in the individual and confine the human race to restoring equilibrium as soon as possible by reinstating what had always been.

There is no progress without risk and risk is costly. Often the individual must pay the price of change for the multitude. I do not intend here to defend BPD insofar as it is a disorder. I only wish to point out that what we collectively define as disordered is somewhat relative to the demands of the times and the consensus of the many when viewing the experiences of the few. Genius must by definition probe the depths and many people with BPD have done so.

Shame is often the shadow that pursues those who for whatever reason find that they have taken an un-mapped course into the wilderness of their own being. It is no small part of therapy to point out that those who suffer from mental illnesses may be less alone than they imagine they are. Historical precedent is often the best place to look for comfort. Many great authors of the past may have written of BPD though only centuries later would it be given a name. What have been termed Axis Two Personality Disorders in the Diagnostic and Statistical Manual are more a matter of degree than of kind. The difficulties that Borderlines have in coping with life are common to all humankind. It is by making common cause with those who seem most unlike us that we realize that the madness that surrounds us is within us as well.

Even men of such stature as the great Doctor Samuel Johnson of Litchfield and London would, if magically transported through time, appear to be a virtual compendium of mental disorders. Johnson manifested signs of depression, anxiety, various tics and compulsions, and various phobias. To suffer from BPD then need not entail discouragement, still less despair. The current therapies are daily being supplemented by new research and most people with BPD will grow beyond the criteria that once led to their diagnosis. The modulation of mood-swings is the fruit of maturity in confrontation with the challenges of life. It takes time to escape the desire to prematurely conclude that the theme and content of any human life can be definitively known. Only art is able to reach the closure and perfection that many Borderlines believe are required in order to be human and to possess value. Humor, humility, and time teach us otherwise.

The knowledge of the suffering of others becomes part of what each of us must live with each day. Deaths and catastrophes are ubiquitous. Our world has made a degree of not-knowing a prerequisite for self-preservation. To entertain a universal sympathy in a global village exhausts our reserves of compassion. The knowledge that such a troubling syndrome as BPD exists is often met with the question, "Why should I care?" This of course presumes that BPD sufferers are merely petulant children as though being petulant and demanding was not what distinguishes the human race itself. If we were happy with our condition we would be like the race of the species of gorilla, happily munching vegetation and grooming each other in the tropical rain-forests of Rwanda, rather than building cities, constructing economies, and writing books. Borderlines can be seen from this perspective as human ... only more so.

Still, we are living in a world of scarce resources, a world that is impatient even with those who are struggling to bear their own weight and make some contribution to the common enterprise of collective survival in precarious times. The question must arise then why a vast and growing literature should exist addressed to helping individuals who are as challenging and self-destructive as are those who manifest symptoms of BPD?

It is no accident that when males are diagnosed with BPD that violence often takes the place of verbal rage and tears. Incarceration often takes the place of various therapeutic settings for males with BPD. Our society is more tolerant of mood swings when manifested by women. BPD is often assumed to be only normal femininity multiplied logarithmically to a higher power. Such women in prior ages would simply have been termed difficult or hysterical by those who needed to deal with them. Our social expectations no longer speak of hysteria but of various forms of depression as endemic among women who are "highly strung" or "high maintenance." We rename old syndromes and think by doing so to understand them better.

Many movie stars appear to have manifested the characteristics of BPD. It is currently even fashionable to be immature, vain, and suspicious of others while asking for immoderate concessions left and right while flying from one exotic location to another if you can afford to do so. It is easy to forget among the merely petulant that there are those for whom BPD is an actual mental disorder and perhaps a disease with at least some basis in organic brain structures. To negotiate with a disease implies a freedom that may not be present and to blame people who are already suffering is not only arbitrary but insensitive if not cruel.

Yet, this book presumes that our common humanity retains some measure of choice even when freedom is compromised and diminished by mental illness. We exist in a world of cause and effect and though the linkages are not always just or proportionate they provide some sense that we can rely upon the world and not assume that blind chance rules the day. By tightening the linkages and making manifest the latent connectivity between actions and results some of the "slack" in cause and consequence is diminished in BPD and instances of magical-thinking are replaced by a zone of limited but real freedom.

Still, it is not surprising that many people fail to negotiate the trials of psychological development whether those that are described by Erik Erickson's eight stages of human development or Abraham Maslow's stages of self-actualization. Not all of us reach emotional maturity. Even while theorists like Kernberg, Winnicott, Kohut, and Masterson have advanced our knowledge of what may be the basis for the observed symptoms of BPD, much research still remains to be completed. New therapies promise hope for better functioning but the question remains of how resources shall be allocated when a condition is as massively disabling and pervasive as BPD appears at times to be.

If part of contract negotiation is the initial bargaining power of each party to the contract, then persons with BPD would appear to enter the process of negotiation at a decided disadvantage. Adequate motivation for growth often seems lacking. But in this case the ultimate beneficiary of the contract is the Borderline person herself. Pointing this out may lessen resistance and create willingness to change. In any case the instincts of all right-thinking persons must be to help her to alleviate the degree of unnecessary suffering that characterizes BPD.

Only someone who has seen the world from the bottom of the well can imagine how dim is the tiny circle of blue sky floating high above or how hard it is to scale the dripping walls and to regain the world she has lost. Sounds of life float down and various cries for help may ascend but years may pass with little progress made. There will be setbacks, but it is my profound hope that the deep distress of BPD itself may summon aid even when frustration and premature surrender may be met with time and again. The real task of adjustment is to instill courage, patience, and a profoundly realistic and flexible repertoire of responses in the patient so that the Borderline can mourn and then abandon the futility of sacrificing her future in the cause of past poor choices made and lost opportunities now regretted. Let them go.

This advice is not meant to diminish or to minimize the suffering or injustices that may have led a person to adopt over time the BPD solution. What I am suggesting is that to allow the past to continually infect the future only serves to compound past injuries by colluding with the conditions that have proved to be obstacles to growth. To deny the past only drives the pain further underground but to allow the past to create a hegemonic grasp upon the present and to forestall all intentionality is to stifle the life force that allows us to surpass and surmount past deficits. It is time to seek re-admission to the same world in which we all must exist together as best we may through resignation and determination.

Much has been written regarding the many ways that psychic pain becomes structured within the body and the most successful psychotherapeutic schools and practices are purgative and devoted to uncovering the past by providing an opportunity for sharing with at least one sympathetic witness what has hitherto been confined in the isolation chambers of our souls. Healing usually requires a dyadic process of communication, a sharing that was once impossible because to do so was only to invite further injury. Much of borderline acting-out may be a symbolic portrayal of what has happened. As the signifying symptoms yield to openness and new perspectives change can happen and new skills can be mastered. Love and balanced supportiveness will often play no small role in BPD therapy as in life. Trust is a life-long pursuit in an uncertain world. Trust is the fruit of sustained love. Love is patient, kind, and takes no offense; it endures all things, hopes all things, and often finds that it can indeed achieve miracles.

Postscript:

I Fall to Pieces

Two of the author's favorite songs are *"Total Eclipse of the Heart"* sung by Bonnie Tyler and *"Landslide"* sung by Stevie Nicks. The lyrics of both describe an experience that most persons with BPD will readily recognize of feeling that they are falling apart and unable to cope with the demands placed upon them by a world that cannot understand the nature or proportionality in the Borderline's responses to fairly common life-stressors.

At such times the person with BPD may lose her sense of possessing an ego with boundaries that tell her who she is. She may feel devalued and betrayed and quite literally alienated from her familiar surroundings and associates to a degree that is usually only seen in cases of extreme dissociation or even psychosis. These episodes of intense distress may be quite temporary and she may emerge from them almost as though she were a sleeper awakening from a dream where for a time at least everything was inverted and dreadful. No rationalization can deny that for a time at least her usually competent self was out of commission and she was living in a state of profoundly altered consciousness – she was falling apart. Borderlines tend to live from crisis to crisis with intermittent periods of what would be termed adequate functioning. The problem is one of intense fragility and a tendency to a flight of ideas. Small inputs may trigger trains of symbolic association that can advance a small incident into a vast and unsubstantiated set of generalizations. Borderlines live in a world where transmutations are common where security and stability require constant vigilance and where outside forces may suddenly penetrate the well-guarded perimeter to the inner compound where she seeks to maintain her sense of solace and self-worth.

BPD carries with it a set of abilities that in any other circumstance would be considered talents. The constant vigilance of others that they maintain and the acute sensitivity to even the slightest gradation of judgment, disapproval, or scorn from other people means that a Borderline can be selectively but accurately insightful. Their passions make them interesting and even fatally fascinating to others. Many are artistic or persuasive. Their suspicions may have given them gifts for acting or dissimulation in order to get by in daily life. When under control of strong emotions they may carry all before them because people hesitate to upset them further or to oppose their intense desires. They may even appear to be dictatorial and the very last people to experience intense self-doubts or loathing; yet these remarkable people are often their own worst enemies. They proceed from crisis to crisis and can turn the slightest provocation into grounds for intense drama. An intense search immediately begins for a culprit or responsible party and the Borderline may alternate swiftly from an intensely felt hatred and condemnation of other people and then with equal facility apply these same standards to themselves. Borderlines live in constant dread that what is good in their lives will be snatched away. Opposite states of feeling and judgment are not reached by a process of gradual attrition but with lightening-like speed without having to first to traverse a middle-ground in transition. This habit of mind is extremely confusing to others who do not share it. They cannot understand what appears to them to be the Borderline's disproportionate distress and extreme reactions to what may from outside seem to be trivial incidents or neutral circumstances. Every effort to reassure the Borderline individual is assumed to be further proof of insensitivity or duplicity and betrayal from significant others. Under these circumstances it becomes difficult to know what to do or say. Even experienced therapists who understand the unique characteristics of Borderline experiences and perceptions are often at a loss for how to best proceed. This only escalates the general level of stress for all concerned. Empathy begins at the point where those who do not suffer from these episodes to imagine what it is like to live with them on a frequent basis. Borderlines are not always in these dreadful emotional storms and it is this very fact that makes it appear to other people to be random or willful by the Borderline when such incidents do occur.

Persons with BPD have times when just nothing seems to help. A job loss, a break-up in a significant relationship, an encounter that is significantly demeaning, or any other of "the thousand shocks that flesh is heir to" may set the first snows in motion that may grow to avalanche proportions with surprising rapidity. The function of a supportive therapist or a network of friends is to be there at these critical times to offer temporary life-support until the storm system moves through and the blue skies return. If a person with BPD in crisis is thought of as similar to any other acute condition that profoundly alters our everyday sense of self it will be possible to understand what Borderlines go through when in a meltdown. The word "meltdown" is usually applied to the consequences of an out of control chain-reaction in a nuclear-power generating facility. When we apply this term to a person with BPD it refers to various out of control emotional states from panic attacks to episodes of intense anger.

The term "containment," one also drawn from a nuclear origin, means to re-establish some sense of proportion, balance, control, and stability when the Borderline is reacting to various situational cues that have set off a chain of reactive emotion within her. There is evidence that a physiological basis for the intense emotions that persons with BPD experience. It is possible that what is involved is analogous to the way that a microphone may exhibit what is called feedback. Each wave of emotion triggers similar incidents through a process of association until the Borderline person begins to feel that she cannot cope with the waves of feeling that are breaking in upon her.

The result is a series of maladaptive and impulsive acts that are engaged in as a desperate measure to reassert control or to restore some measure of equilibrium and regain confidence that she can cope with things. This sense of adequate coping with a problematic issue in turn helps persons with BPD to regulate their self-esteem issues. When a Borderline feels that she is not coping effectively or meeting her own often unrealistically strict standards she often feels intense shame or guilt. These feelings in turn only add to the mix of unpleasant feelings and the result is a meltdown.

The world of the Borderline is one where daily life is lived on a precarious edge between vague anxiety and complete panic. The swift alternations in emotional valences combined with a set of beliefs that are often at variance with ordinary social conventions make Borderlines demanding and helpless in ways that appear to be assumed rather than real. Their behavior may appear childlike or worse, as the behavior of a spoiled and demanding child. Many persons with BPD have chronically reached the limits of their acquired containment efforts and as a result can be overwhelmed by certain stimuli or situations that most people manage to take in stride without undue upsets let alone a complete meltdown. A useful analogy to this experience is seen in geology when a heavy rainfall can result in a hillside becoming water-logged so that a sort of colloidal suspension of soil particles results. This can lead to landslides of what had hitherto appeared to be stable hillsides. Even when the Borderline's behavior is most histrionic however it is not put on or assumed for the occasion. The feelings of panic, betrayal, and emotional vertigo are real.

We all assume that our world is anchored like a spider web at various significant points so that our sense of basic existential security is maintained and sustainable. Persons with BPD can feel at times that their entire world is threatened because of a sneering comment from a stranger, a moment of abruptness or dismissal from a friend, or if they have a brush with the law such as a routine traffic stop. Suddenly the Borderline is overwhelmed with a pervasive and all encompassing sense of shame or terror. Everything appears unstable and familiar surroundings may appear alien, menacing, and even horrifying.

As the feelings of meltdown escalate the patient with BPD will begin to thrash about for a solution, to get things to come again into focus, to re-establish a sense of control even if only symbolic means are available. Much of Borderline aggressiveness is due to their propensity to launch a pre-emptive strike before being shamed or abandoned. Borderlines often attribute accidental or thoughtless actions by others as facets of a comprehensive and multifaceted plot to starve them into submission or to reduce them to a state of utter helplessness and dependency prior to being abandoned.

Granted their experiences and their intense reactivity to fear or stress these thoughts are less delusional than they would otherwise appear. One of the primary aims of this book has been to help people who do not have these dreadful experiences or reverberating reactions to understand and to empathize with people who do. Only then will their reputation for willfulness, duplicity, and outrageous behavior be revealed as frantic efforts to deal with chaotic perceptions and an overwhelming sense that either they or the universe are evil and out of tune and probably both simultaneously. Rapid and total revaluations may take place; persons who have previously been idealized as saviors or all-powerful protectors may suddenly be seen as utter frauds and as worthless should they fail to respond on cue and as expected during a Borderline's frequent and recurring crises. Everyone is potentially on call and presumed to be instantly available on demand to get the Borderline through a really bad spell – diva, darling, waif, or ravaging vampire, the Borderline in crisis may slide through various roles with the facility of a musician practicing the scales.

These are not however mere modes of manipulation. The Borderline is carried along as in many ways only one more observer of the stampede of her thoughts, feelings, and representations when her inner-world is in crisis. She is convinced that things will keep accelerating until they cannot be stopped unless she does something desperate. When seen from this angle certain actions that help her attain focus and balance such as focalized acts of cutting make total sense even if they are harmful. Borderlines often feel a need to make small sacrifices to avoid more extensive losses just as the losses incurred by forest fires may be minimized by a prior controlled burn.

In a Borderline's meltdowns the innate human fight or flight responses usually get triggered and certain places and people may be suddenly blanketed in a fog of mistrust and suspicion. An intense emotional charge like static electricity builds up and must be discharged. It is then that the Borderline lashes out. Only a complete and all encompassing solution is perceived to be adequate. The Borderline need to reassert control and to reinstate her self-esteem may at such times seem so essential and her need to take some action so desperate that she may put her life or the lives of others at risk. She may tear apart relations of long standing, suddenly quit a job or decide to move, or make other life-altering decisions without forethought or consideration. Impulsive suicidal actions may occur or she may court accidents through reckless or self-punitive actions. The short-term and situation dependent psychotic episodes that sometimes occur with Borderlines are also linked with these experiences of meltdown and the resulting identity diffusion.

The professional consensus among most mental-health workers is that persons who suffer from BPD manifest a disorder of object-relations in the self and in others. This means that these patients often find it impossible to prevent problems in communication because of a perceptual tendency for the subjects to be perceived differently over time through a process called splitting. Sudden transpositions of affect can occur based on some word or action that may trigger an entirely different line of associations that impose their shade upon the current transaction. To deal with someone who has BPD is like trying to engage with a moving target. It may require years of therapy to heal the fractured personality elements that persons with BPD use daily to encounter the world. Absent a consistent frame of reference the very terms of a contract may need to be renegotiated because for the Borderline even the smallest lacunae will allow room for contention and dispute. Basic mistrust based on shifting perceptual fields places the Borderline in a position of fighting a guerilla war with the world.

Another useful image might be that of a movie with many production difficulties due to a constantly altered script, temperamental actors, and a difficult director. There are constant delays, frustration all round, and little to show in the rushes at the end of the day. But in this case many of the roles from writer to director are played by the Borderline herself. Other persons get auditioned as extras to the drama but they are replaceable. They come and go while the drama remains basically the same from year to year. No final product ever emerges from the film editor. The weary production simply grinds along from year to year and some distant executive or board of directors may keep the film in production rather than folding it up and just taking a loss. BPD is not the only example of the vanity of human wishes but it may be one of the least rewarding for all parties concerned.

But we are not really talking about metaphors here; we are talking about a human life. Giving up is not an option but neither is simply giving in to every demand the Borderline may make. The goal is to contain the illness to the degree that this is possible and to minimize its deleterious effects. The search for a framework for experience is provided for most of us from two sources: the nature of the objective world in which we live, what psychologists call reality-testing, and by the scarcity of human resources and a general unwillingness to allow one party to dictate terms in the countless transactions of everyday life. The approach that this book has taken is that the very framing of experience and stability that borderline persons seek is ready to hand. Reality and the scarcity of resources are the containment vehicles that can provide a structure for the Borderline's life.

Since the person with BPD will always find it possible to question the good intentions of other people as she bounces back and forth between idealization and devaluation it may be best to keep relations at a studied level of superficiality, conclude the transaction, and move on. By reducing each life-transaction to a dimension where strict performance can be objectively ascertained conflicts regarding the quality of the relationship can be minimized. Personal qualities and motivations can never be reduced to a substance or a single act because these are tendencies and directions not final ends to be reached once and for all. They are never finally attained or attainable. In the search for perfect validation or perfect rejection the borderline individual exhausts her life energies and drives other persons to distraction. Only by surrendering superlatives can she find what actual happiness may be possible for her in her one limited life in a world that will not alter quickly enough to match her many demands and expectations.

This is not to say that the borderline quest for the ideal is always misplaced. Love is the transcendent end that is implanted within us simply by being human. What I am arguing for here is a temporary suspension of the quest for the ideal world that she so desires to make up for past losses so as to make room for and to build confidence over time in achieving through an inductive manner successful human interactions experienced one at a time.

This adjusted settlement with life implies the need to see each day as an opportunity to enter a process of negotiation in order to reach, not a perfect or once-and-for-all solution, but rather an optimal solution for all parties to the current limited transaction. Despair and the resulting effort at subjugation to prevent abandonment is not the solution; neither is the pursuit of complete and arbitrary control of significant others ever possible. When she asks for more than reality can supply the Borderline risks losing everything. Negotiation to meet our wants and needs appears to be a universal imperative. To entertain the possible as a substitute for the perfect is the beginning of healing.

Why then do those with BPD seem unable to reconcile themselves with human limitations? Is it perhaps because some early deficit in adequate mirroring has left them feeling every deprivation as though it were abysmal and a threat to their very existence? Many theorists have taken this line of reasoning and looked to early abuse or failure to negotiate certain critical periods in object-relation development as the cause of BPD. Others have suggested that BPD manifests a temperamental or affective illness, one where the aggressive or oral impulses are unbalanced and demanding. Others still have related BPD to schizophrenia and to a breakdown in reality testing in what amounts to intermittent bouts of psychosis.

I suggest that these inquiries, however much they may guide research, will not answer to the current needs and wants of a person with BPD who may remain clinically ill for some time. Unless she is hospitalized she will need to manage in the world to some degree. Our current policies towards the mentally ill are far from ideal. This means that our society has placed much of the responsibility of getting by back onto the mentally ill person herself. However lamentable this may be it is best to face the fact that the borderline quest for a perfect match between what she desires and perhaps even at times deserves to expect will not be universally forthcoming. She may have to compromise and to forego the perfect mirroring that she may desire. By surrendering the search for acceptable motivations in other people and resting content with mere adequate performance on reasonable terms she may reach an optimal solution to daily transactions and over time become more reconciled to the demands of reality as a result of this process.

This is what it means to negotiate with the borderline personality as a life configuration that otherwise may prove intractable and will bring about results that are far worse than any compromise that I have advocated here will bring. Whether negotiation and consent are possible in any specific case remains an open question of course. Human freedom is never perfect. The best way to proceed appears to be to entertain hope, the one virtue that, because it is always future oriented, is always available no matter how many prior disappointments may have occurred. It is in this spirit that that this book is presented to its future readers. The same intense reactivity that is present in persons with BPD often has an upside as well. Their delight and joy is often as impressive as their more negative feelings and makes them delightful to be with just as a sunny day can bring out all of the beauty of a rugged coastline.

Taking life with both the bitter and the sweet is a phrase applicable to dealing with this unique variety of human experience as is the advice of my grandaunt who lived to be over one-hundred years old, "Life isn't too bad all in all if you don't weaken."

Or to take one last nautical; analogy: Keep to the last course charted when clouds appear on the horizon or the barometer starts to drop. Heave-to for a while if necessary, put your sea-anchor out, take the oncoming waves on the bow, and let the storm blow itself out. Don't weaken; hang in there; you are worth it. It is possible to negotiate with Borderline Personality Disorder with persistence and good faith, with patience and understanding, with imagination and foresight, and finally with empathy and with love.

Appendix

Note: Only after consultation with the primary therapist as to the propriety and timing of the use of these brief editorial notes, comments, and suggestions in the appendices (and whether they may be employed at all in any specific case) should the following be considered and employed in dealing with anyone with BPD.

In order to help in the negotiation process the following guidelines may be of help. A mistrustful and even adversarial stance may be presumed at first in dealing with someone with BPD. The defenses of projection, projective identification, and splitting are primitive psychological tactics but they are effective simply because they tend to subvert all discussion and preclude compromises.

For this reason it must be made clear that something valued by the Borderline person will be unavailable in the future absent some effort at change and that reasonable conditions will be imposed, not out of some punitive desire but in the interests of the ongoing relationship and that both parties will benefit by reaching an agreement. Unilateral victories have in fact made the world of the Borderline insupportable and survival demands some degree of flexibility.

This will come as a shock to the Borderline and will tend to elicit panic and accusations of betrayal at first but the end result will open a gap through which light and air can penetrate into what has become a stale and menaced existence. The essence of a contract is offer and acceptance. By previously mapping out emotional triggers and the course of Borderline responses in a flow chart some degree of insight may have already been reached by both parties. This insight defines the initial bargaining positions.

Threats should be avoided since negotiation requires some degree of calm from both parties. The positive aspects of bargaining should be emphasized. It is not that former benefits will be taken away; they are already gone. Further compliance with Borderline demands is now contingent on their reasonableness and can only be reached through the bargaining process. This must be made clear in a gentle but firm manner. It is imperative that no hidden vengefulness or punitive intent be present and that a ruthless purging take place of any co-dependent or self-justified feelings in the non-borderline person.

Each party may be invited to express the ideal position that they would entertain if all of their demands were to be met, but it must be understood that some flexibility will be demanded from each party. The contract will restore ideally a middle ground that has been absent or that was lost somewhere along the way during the course of the relationship. By defining this middle-ground by an ever more refined process of negotiation, one of offer and acceptance, both parties are brought back to relations from the cliff-edge of rejection and abandonment and the defeat that such an outcome would represent for each of them.

Offers should be conditionally worded as in:

I propose this if you will do that.

Or alternatively:

If you are willing to do this, then I will reciprocate with that.

If an offer is unacceptable as stated then a counter-offer may be proposed. This cycle can go back and forth for some time and may become more refined as the negotiation process goes on. If after a reasonable time no agreement is reached, then a stalemate in negotiations should be recognized and the bargaining should cease for now and be postponed to some time in the future that is agreeable to both parties. If the discussion should become heated on either side, then it is no longer a negotiation but an exchange of threats. Discussion must cease until a more suitable occasion offers. There should be no illusion that negotiation is a zero-sum game with a winner and a loser. Negotiation presumes that each party has something to gain or to lose and that the bargained-for-exchange will be value-maximizing for both.

It is precisely the presumption that one party is perfectly healthy and the other perfectly ill that results in what I have called the Borderline Situation, a state of affairs that requires two or more people to sustain it. To illustrate this, a person marooned on a desert island might still be diagnosable as manifesting symptoms of BPD but absent some other person on the island the Borderline Situation would not be possible except in reminiscence. It is true that people with BPD are often engaged in processing old wounds but without interaction of some sort this is a solitary activity and unless mirrored by another equally engaged it is like sending semaphore signals out into the darkness when no ship is in sight.

This book presumes that we live in a shared world, what phenomenological psychologists call the Mitwelt of human relations. The alternative to negotiation is the issuance of unilateral demands that must finally fail because they elicit resistance. Once this is recognized by defining the bargaining posture of each party communication and compromise replaces appropriation, threats, intimidation, and even violence. Absent agreement eventual severance and mutual loss will be inevitable. Paradoxical victories by mutual suffering may seem to offer relief but only in a fashion that inverts reward and punishment and mocks human intelligence and the possibility of true reward and happiness. To such unanswerable folly history is the lamentable witness, but it is always to be met with incomprehension as senseless and unnecessary and therefore to be rejected.

This is not to blame the person with BPD but rather to understand that there are limits to the ability of anyone to witness and share the degree of chaos that can break out in what may appear to be minor human interactions when BPD is present. Whatever its origins across and within various social contexts the BPD life-script is a source of anguish, one so deeply rooted that every perception takes on the tenor and quality of the inner experience of the borderline individual. BPD is a trigger for whatever dysfunctions may be present in virtually any environment. It acts as a sort of universal catalyst on other people, one that dissolves the sense of competency and the inner sense of integrity of persons who witness or share in the proximity of BPD.

This is what makes this particular disorder so challenging and so prone to instill various counter-transference reactions in therapy. The danger to the integration and self-worth of other people is extreme and often the only sensible course to prevent things from spiraling beyond repair is to entrust persons with BPD to others who are more able to respond to them in an adequate manner.

I think that the basic borderline position could be summed up as one based on resentment and the upholding of a very idiosyncratic, high and inflexible sense of what Freud's superego demands for them and for others. When they feel that they measure up to their interior ideal they feel powerful and entitled and when they fail they want to slink away or throw themselves on the mercy of other people who they temporarily idealize.

In addition, Borderlines like to hand out sentences of exile or capital punishment and pardons in the Borderline's world are few. Their quick and even hair-trigger perceptions are often accurate as far as they go but what is lacking is perspective and the ability to realize that very few things in human life are constants let alone absolutes. Borderlines demand a variety of prairie-justice where no circuit-riding judge is required and justice is meted out quickly and without allowing the accused to waste time in final words to the court before judgment is passed.

Borderlines spend a considerable amount of time contemplating or arranging various exit scenarios. This can be seen in the life and death of Marilyn Monroe who manifested many of the symptoms that at the present time are used to diagnose Borderline Personality Disorder. She combined many contrasting states depending upon whether she felt powerful, entitled, and in control or whether she felt lost, abandoned, unworthy, and flawed. She would seek refuge in her dressing room and only emerge with great reluctance when filming.

Even when she condescended to come out she would often require multiple takes and would often forget her lines. She was such a trial to various directors that few wanted to work with her again. She was renowned for her chronic lateness and unreliability so that it was something of a joke when she sang Happy Birthday to President Kennedy to be referred to by Peter Lawford as "the late Marilyn Monroe." By a few months later in August of 1962 it was the only way to refer to her because she was in fact dead, dead by suicide.

It was largely a matter of unfortunate timing that she died when she did. She had lived for so long on the edge with barbiturates for years. Why was it different now? This was not her first overdose but this time she had just been essentially fired from her studio which was in its own process of radical reappraisal after sustained economic losses. She had been acting especially erratically at the time even for her and perhaps she felt that her sexually shady past was returning as the only way to obtain notice and validation. She was already entering the period when biology begins the slow withdrawal of its former largess and youthful beauty begins to wane. Her long evasive quest to escape her dreadful childhood and her mother's mental illness had seemed to come full circle and she may have felt as alone and abandoned as she had been then.

That final night her psychiatrist was going out at precisely a time when her sense of radical solitude seemed most insupportable. The wheel spun and the wrong number came up this time. She ran out of chances. Cycles of provocative behavior, long rooted addictions, and an ego that had been fed everything but what it really required, consistent love for being nothing more or less special than being just one other complex and imperfect human being had finally done her in. All efforts to disrupt her various dysfunctions had failed. All efforts to love her somehow had come up short of her incessant demands.

Nothing was enough for Marilyn Monroe so what about the other Borderlines who are often asked to make do with so much less? The answer is that it is not a question of more: more drugs, more sex, more fame, a different lover, or anything else than to change the basic faulty life-orientation away from the terminal aloneness, specialness, and exceptionalism whether good or bad that Borderlines feel about themselves. The urge to take various premature exits to re-establish a sense of power and control should be replaced by a commitment to stay the course of therapy, of healing, and of commitment to life. The essential and enduring should be retained and the multitude of temporary fixes resisted or at least replaced bit by bit with a lasting sense of her essential dignity and worth as a human being.. It takes a new operating system and not just a change of software for lasting improvement. It means dethroning the queen, breaking the hermit out of her solitude, and helping the lost child to trust the process of recovery even if she still harbors doubts about individual people in her life.

The *"I will leave you before you can leave me"* dynamic is common in the course of BPD. In order to make the connections of the story work a borderline person will frame a scenario that inverts cause and effect and uses projection and projective identification to assign to others what are the Borderline's own emotions and actions. Here are some examples with the real meaning explained in parentheses:

You hate me. (I am doing things to you that if done to me by you would arouse feelings of hatred in me so you must hate me/ or/ I hate you right now so you must in turn hate me).

Never contact me again. (I just came back to give you a chance to see that I expect you to read my hidden message that although I really feel like I never want to see or hear from you again I am also very lonely and wish that you could show me how I can be angry with someone without taking unilateral action to end longstanding or valuable relationships).

You wouldn't leave me if you knew how much I have put into this relationship; no one else will do as much for you as I have. (I am the one who is leaving but I want you to be responsible for my decision because I doubt the wisdom of what I am doing).

You are completely self-centered and narcissistic. (I hate it when you remind me of the things that I hate most in myself – my desperate need for mirroring and confirmation from others).

I am so tired of hearing what you are doing. (If I compliment you it will be to my loss because life is always a zero-sum game. If you think you are really something, then you are almost certain to eventually leave me because I often feel like I am nothing and unworthy to even live).

I am going to kill myself because you want me to die. (I want to die because I would rather not do what it takes to get well and I want it to be your fault because I have no control of my actions but magically you do have such control).

You think you're so perfect. (You make me feel that I am nothing because of the judgment that I pass on myself).

You seem so self-sufficient and able to meet all your own needs. (I feel empty and unable to generate my own joy and I attribute to you perfection instead of seeing you as just another human being with needs and failings. When you seem most perfect I need to knock you down to the level where I feel on an equal level with you; of course if I succeed in this I will ask myself why I am wasting my time with you).

You are a lousy therapist! (I'm afraid that you are asking me to heal, even though I came to you for help. If I would try, I just might get better. But then I am afraid of what it might mean to be healthy! After all, by being sick I can shift all my problems to others and make it their fault when I mess up).

Your insights aren't telling me anything that I don't already know! (But knowing it has never made a difference; I just don't know how to control my shifting feelings and my impulsive actions).

Help me! But by tomorrow I'll be back to feeling like the queen of the universe needing no one at all. (I'm the queen the universe but all the while I feel like nothing inside).

You'll never understand me! (I take pride in being always one step ahead of anyone who even tries to understand and help me).

Borderlines can play both sides of the net of their psychic tennis match with the world; everyone else is really just a set of spectators or witnesses. BPD leads (if not arrested) to one outcome: the destruction of the Borderline herself ... game, set, match!

The first goal to achieve then with someone with BPD is to try and ensure her survival. The severe mental pain and feelings of being worthless or abandoned tends to deprive persons with BPD of the horizon provided by past trials that have been successfully navigated to augment their current coping skills. Whatever she is currently feeling appears to be necessary, inevitable, permanent, and without a remedy. The aggression that normally serves a survival function can then be turned back upon the self with disastrous and irremediable consequences. It is important to recall at such times how swiftly moods have changed in the past and by waiting it out and reaching out it is possible to make it through whatever is currently causing her feelings of anger, terror, or emotional confusion.

Just letting everything go with an, "I just don't care anymore attitude," or "This will show them," or "Who cares about me anyway?" is a case of substituting actions for impulses. Say it; don't do it.

Persons with BPD can separate or dissociate at times and view their body or life without compassion. This tendency to identify with a persecutory aspect of themselves can be dangerous to their survival.

Part of the mapping out of danger zones and past traumas that tend to be re-lived is to prepare in advance of meltdowns a list of danger areas to be avoided and also to make a list of coping strategies to get ready in advance for when predictable triggers have started the emotional domino effect so common in BPD.

Understand "Borderline Bleed," a tendency for emotions to proceed under their own momentum, sometimes in free-fall until they meet an opposing force. Quick re-evaluations of relationships of long standing can occur when persons with BPD feel neglected, rejected, or misunderstood.

Be prepared for quick switching between alternative ego-states in persons with BPD. Panic, suspicion, feelings of desolation, or anger can appear seemingly out of a clear blue sky and only by letting them pass and then gently tracing the chain backwards can the meaning be revealed link by link.

Many people with BPD live in a state of hair-trigger alert even when they seem relaxed and are having a good time. Massive inversions or evaluations of views can be triggered by small inputs. Cause and effect are often vastly different in degree. Happiness and trust are often held in suspicion and reversal is often presumed so that defenses can be immediately deployed. This explains why so many persons with BPD avoid situations where there are too many stimuli and why social situations can prove overwhelming to them. The need to retreat to safe ground can lead to a hermit-like existence.

The need for surveillance and control can simply exhaust the inner resources of someone with BPD. The habit of retrospection and review can tend to spoil even happy occasions when they are later replayed for hidden meanings or motives. Sources of ordinary embarrassment can seem to be great failures bringing excruciating shame.

Therapists learn swiftly that successful communication with someone with BPD may require them to ignore various provocative gestures and to deftly side-step various traps that the Borderline may lay for them. There is a "gamey" quality to BPD and playing the game is an acquired skill. The defense called projective identification involves one of these tactics. The Borderline will suddenly launch an attack to see if the party against whom it is being directed will buy into the guilt or other negative feelings that are being beamed at them as if from a laser. The object from the point of view of the Borderline is to equalize the stakes. Feeling as persons with BPD so often do that everyone else is "put together" but them it becomes natural to launch a preemptive strike to restore what they view as equality. *"Why should I be the only one who feels bad? It just isn't fair!"*

If the communication is not clear or seems as though it has been "mined" with a BPD version of an Improvised Exploding Device, then several options are open: To ignore the trap and walk around it by saying something positive; to seek clarification; or not to respond at all to the provocation. Silence is often the best policy because at some level the person with BPD knows what she is doing. By not playing the game the Borderline is stalemated and she has to return to direct communication of her needs and wants rather than using manipulation or resorting to self-destructive gestures.

Her dictatorial entitlement covers emptiness at the core. It is an example of bluff, pretense, and over-kill in action. The hidden message is: *"Why do I have to act-up in order to get your attention; don't you know how lonely and desperate I am?"*

Similarly a Borderline can shift back into helplessness and frantic appeals for aid. Here the task is to remind her of her basic dignity and underutilized powers and abilities. Once the storm passes she will be alright. This is the task of supportive therapy.

A person with BPD can easily get side-tracked into various areas of "odd thinking." Though basic reality-testing remains intact they may suffer from what might be termed "focal delusions" that are based on overwhelming feelings or symbolic associations. These will melt like ice in the sun if gently confronted once the crisis period is past. It is important to understand that persons with BPD often live with fragmented and unmapped areas of experience, each bearing its own emotional charge and valence. Memories when evoked can carry much of the power that they did when they were initially experienced.

Borderlines tend to believe that inadvertent sleights are planned insults or instances of neglect and of failure to care for and to validate them. Symbols and objects often speak a private language to the Borderline and carry talismanic power or omens of future events for good or ill.

Nothing is ever finally past and laid to rest. Old issues and hurts tend to recur with cumulative weight assigned to them.

Persons with BPD are subject to feeling like different people depending upon whom they are with. This can be disconcerting because it feels like once a relationship becomes maimed in any way then restoration to what it was becomes difficult. Borderlines tend to cycle new relationships as past relationships fall into ruin.

Meetings are stressful because of the risks involved. Borderlines tend to fear their own tendency to "spoil things." Isolation is often the only way that a Borderline person can feel emotionally intact. The gaze and evaluation of others can seem to be insupportable.

Many female borderline patients may rely upon only the body to spare them the tasks imposed by real intimacy. This can lead to habits of promiscuity.

There is a calculus of control and confrontation in even casual encounters so that persons with BPD are often irritable with casual contacts in the course of daily dealings with drivers, salespersons, waitresses, etc. These encounters may be accompanied by feelings of being evaluated and judged by people. Nothing is seen as merely casual, impersonal, and insignificant.

The contentious nature of persons with BPD is a natural outgrowth of their basic lack of trust in other people. Making commitments is notoriously difficult for them because their own experience of themselves has taught them to expect rapid re-evaluations of assessments, plans, and pursuits.

It should always be kept in mind that in many ways persons with BPD live in a mindset that asks the same awkward questions that children ask. Their lack of integration into what is expected of most people and their willingness to live "on the edge" means that they have withheld their consent to many aspects of what most people simply assume is the background assent that is necessary for living in our less than perfect world. It is precisely this radical questioning that can at times make persons with BPD so sensitive and insightful.

Agoraphobia like symptoms may arise when confronted by too many stimuli. Crowds, large cities, noise, and other inputs may overwhelm the coping abilities of the moment for someone with BPD. This leads to a close monitoring of their lives so that their capacities are not overwhelmed.

Symbolic means of undoing or redeeming past failures or bad experiences may cause a person with BPD to use items with talismanic significance to restore equilibrium. Segregating or sacrificing contaminated objects may seem imperative to limit the diffusion of feelings of invasion or spoliation.

All of the above points are meant to show that daily experience for a person with BPD is never simple or unquestioned. It is as though she is engaged in mulling over an obscure manuscript for hidden meanings day by day. Ambiguities must be resolved but even the language employed is always changing. Threats of various sorts are always present, not least those impulses that arise from within her. The body becomes a stage upon which various dramas of inner significance may be enacted. This can take the form of various eating disorders.

The function of cutting, eating disorders, and impulsive actions is to use the outer to signify and express what is occurring within the inner world. This means that one of the major tasks of therapy is to learn to recognize the various themes that arise, the pressure points and triggers that exist, and favored coping mechanisms when the person with BPD is under particular forms of stress.

Time is virtually simultaneous for persons with BPD. Certain feelings can start an avalanche of similar instances. Anger and terror mount in a storm of perceptions that blot out any assurances to the contrary. Everything becomes charged with a razor-edge of inner pain and all reassurance ebbs away into infinite distance. Only metaphor can grasp what this feels like.

Higher functions and normal perceptions are flooded and the sense of self becomes estranged, drawn out like a thin wire suspended over unfathomable depths. Much of the lives of Borderlines are spent in efforts to avoid these awful moments and hours by seeking out various points of refuge. Once triggered these dreadful upheavals must run their course. The poison seems to infiltrate every association and relationship - anger fear betrayal. All are unworthy of trust; no one understands. The spiked walls arise topped with broken glass. *Let no one enter! Ever!*

The magical thinking and brief psychotic episodes that persons with BPD are said to manifest stem from these periods when perceptual storms carry all before them. The aggressive feelings that arise can be turned against the self in a desperate effort to regain control by making the self into an object. *"When I cut myself it is not really me; there is no me left to feel."*

It is said that by the laws of mathematics and physics certain great waves arise in the ocean that are multiples of the wave trains of which they are a part. Borderlines live on an unguarded ocean where such marauding waves abound. Maybe the greatest fear that Borderlines possess is that somewhere out there is a black mass of water that will submerge everything forever. *What if this time I just don't come back?*

Always remember, you have survived this far. You owe it to yourself to make it just one more time. The same dissociation that allows you to step into the role of the persecutor can make you a sympathetic ally to your beleaguered self. Keep reaching out. You are not alone.

Just as in the case of nations that normally rely upon diplomacy to resolve conflicts, the international equivalent of negotiation in the civil arena, a state of war will sever these relations and substitute the rule of force. Persons with BPD may choose to escalate their demands beyond what any negotiation can contemplate. At this point diplomatic qualities of reason and debate are suspended and action invites a reciprocal response. The problem of course is that absent an immediate threat to self or others our society preserves the sovereignty of the individual and the borderline patient is often adept at concealing symptoms when the occasion requires this degree of duplicity. This means that the prevention of suicide must rest squarely with the patient herself as the only one in a position to meet her illness head-on by opting for life.

This reality is recognized in most treatment contexts and if not provided for early on is usually lamented later when the patient uses emotional blackmail of the highest order to get what she wants. To begin along this path by implying that the burdens of essential life choices may be transferred to another person denies the very reality that it is the goal of therapy to instill in the place of the BPD configuration of traits and dispositions.

The ultimate weapon in the Borderline Arsenal is suicide. Therapists learn early on that suicide for someone with an affective disorder is different than the suicide of someone with BPD. The former may commit suicide out of surrender and despair or to simply bring intolerable suffering to an end. As such the suicide of the depressive is a case of the surrender of control. This is far less likely to be the case with BPD. The suicide of Borderlines has an edge, an aggressive component that implies that suicide can serve a strategic or tactical purpose for them. This means that for the Borderline suicide is not a surrender of control but an overt manifestation of a desire to exercise control at all costs. The fact that success in the endeavor will prevent even the possibility of the satisfaction of having achieved the desired goal seems to elude them. It is like setting a table with a delicious feast and then perishing in mere contemplation of a result that they can never be absolutely sure will unfold as they wish. Vengeance may be muted, sorrow matched with a slow but salutary healing in others, and pity in the survivors moderated by a sense of the sheer waste of a life that might have eventually found succor through insight and humble compliance with a regimen of recovery.

Such a suicide is less an appeal for help than it is a refusal of it. The message is one of anger and assault upon the natural order of things by wanton destruction as a source of final empowerment and control. It is blackmail by other means, extortion by taking the ultimate risk all the while hoping for the big pay-off:

You did this to me; it is all your fault!

It is said that Borderlines are always seeking to use the primitive defenses of denial, projection, and splitting to make other people the focus for what only the Borderline herself can prevent. Nowhere is this truer than in the case of Borderline Suicides. The first element of therapy is to make this clear to the borderline patient – suicide is incompatible with therapy and it is not the job of the therapist to prevent suicidal attempts but rather to explore the dark appeal and fascination that allows the Borderline to engage in a sort of fatal dance with her own destruction. The therapist must not allow the patient to achieve a freedom to behave recklessly by shifting the burden that each of us bears alone: to protect and nurture the life that we have been given and to turn away resolutely from the easy temptation to assume that death is a temporary posture rather than a final and definitive end.

This same analysis is applicable to the other forms of self-destruction, that while stopping short of the immanent endangerment of life, manifest the same spirit of dissociation from the health of mind and body. An example is anorexia nervosa, a condition that often overlaps with BPD. So rewarding does the omnipotent control of the body's weight become for these patients that it becomes irrelevant that their skeletal and aged appearance is a daily demonstration of the fallacy of their idea that inordinate weight loss is an achievement rather than a perverse cycle leading to debility and death.

What drives people to such extremes when, if these measures were inflicted by a regime in a concentration camp, would elicit the outrage of all right thinking people; from whence comes this desperation and fatal distancing of the human personality from its own true best interests? Is it only so that in reading the horror in those who do not share the affliction of BPD the Borderline assumes some God-like role that separates her from the human race? Is it really so terrible to simply accept that we all share a common nature and that the Borderline is neither more than human nor less than human? Instead borderline patients tend to alternate between these two mutually contradictory assessments of their own self-worth and place in the world.

Over time Borderlines in their incessant search for control learn to so anticipate disaster that their gamesmanship requires that they play both sides of the net simultaneously. It is even possible for a bystander to skip a few volleys by simply stepping aside in effect and observing how the battle can continue with no active agency from the one upon whom the Borderline is projecting her current tragic and hateful version of events. If BPD drama was a motion picture it would be noted that when the final credits roll the patient herself was for the most part the writer, the director, and the producer of the film as well as playing the starring role.

The film's title never changes: *Gone with the Wind* or *They Done Me Wrong*. The various imperatives of victimhood always create the same result because the cast members and technical crew become finally interchangeable. The underlying theme of the film also never changes:

*Nobody will ever love me enough, or if he does then he is either not the person that I am really currently am in love with, or if he is then I know that he will leave me. **Just you wait!** For me, nothing ever works out the way it should. I'm just unlucky that way. But they will pay for it, oh just see if they don't!*

And the wheel turns one more time with hurt and pain all round. BPD may be considered as a tributary of what before the modern age was generically called melancholy, that set of afflictions of mind and body that together added up to the sum of human miseries. As this book began with some brief extracts from Robert Burton's famous *"The Anatomy of Melancholy,"* it shall end as well with quotations from classic literature.

Classics are called classics for a reason, because of their perennial appeal as well as their excellence. Human nature never changes. What has troubled us yesterday will trouble us tomorrow. The affliction that humankind is to itself did not wait until the present age before being noted and classified. It has always been the province of art to plumb the soul. It is therefore certain that we have met BPD and the ravages it entails in prior ages.

Sorrow generally takes itself with great seriousness and in doing so casts aside the gentle physic of laughter. Tears for persons with BPD may at times become so habitual that the basin of the ocean seems unable to contain them. Anger can flare up until no occasion is adequate to explain its cause. The faculty of judgment may be so employed that no one can satisfy its extreme demands. The frantic pursuit of perfection has unseated many from what might have been adequate to meet their needs and sufficient to crown their justifiable ambitions.

If balance and containment are the ends to which therapy seeks to bend our habitual afflictions and reconciliation with fate the goal of the virtues that the stoics once advised us to adopt to secure a happy life, then we may all profit from the adornments of life without coveting them. A little happiness may be adequate to our needs and sacrifices born in patience will yield suppleness to the integuments of the soul.

Selection of Poems
That Manifest Some
Parallels to BPD

An entire separate volume could be written seeking to explain some of the reasons behind the gender disparity found in cases of BPD. Perhaps the reason that BPD so often manifests in young adult females is that young women experience a unique set of stress events that lead to BPD or it may be that young women are caught in cycles of divergent social expectations that make it difficult to experience themselves and their impulses as stable, containable, and manageable. Women are often encouraged to find their identities derivatively through their relationships and are encouraged in habits of dependence at the same time that they are made to feel that they should be able to stand alone. Added to the general burden of human maturation are all of the issues that accompany biological conception and the raising of children. The two or three decades of her biological fertility may be intensely competitive economically and socially. Our society places women in positions of conflicting standards and we are as prone to condemn women as we are to idealize them according to current social and sexual norms. None of this is easy. To be the fulcrums of civilization and the targets of various sophisticated advertising campaigns makes woman's historical status problematic in culture after culture.

Poetry and literature in general often hint at or explain things that are otherwise inaccessible to the conscious mind; for this reason I have chosen to conclude this volume with various selections from poems that may convey their own insights into the processes of BPD. I have tried in this book to explore what BPD feels like from inside. I will now close with a selection of various poems that express experiences analogous to those that are often met with in BPD and the familiar and similar sufferings that others in sympathy with them may endure in tandem with those who suffer from this dreadful illness. The elegiac tone of the verses that are included here is not intended to confirm the hopelessness that persons with BPD often feel, but to demonstrate that many great and talented poets have felt similar emotions of anguish and despair and have managed to survive and persevere. BPD is thus not alien to the human equation now matter how alone persons with this diagnosis may feel at times.

Borderline individuals often experience themselves as being terminally unique. One of the best lines in Joseph Conrad's great novel of disgrace and courage, *"Lord Jim,"* tells of the realization by the narrator that Jim was one of us after all. Or again as Walt Whitman once said, "Nothing human is alien to me."

As for those who have been wounded in a relationship with someone with BPD I include the following verses to show them that their experience is also not absent from literature. They are not alone in the dark fascination that they may have experienced with someone with BPD as the poems by Ernest Dowson may demonstrate.

The legacy of a relationship with someone with BPD may require a great deal of time to mourn. As John Keats said in his great poem, *"La Belle Dame sans Merci:"*

I saw their starved lips in the gloam

With horrid warning gaped wide

And I awoke and found me here on the cold hillside

And that is why I sojourn here alone and palely loitering

Though the sedge is withered from the lake

And no birds sing...

I Am

By John Clare

I AM: yet what I am none cares or knows,

My friends forsake me like a memory lost;

I am the self-consumer of my woes,

They rise and vanish in oblivious host,

Like shades in love and death's oblivion lost;

And yet I am, and live with shadows tost

Into the nothingness of scorn and noise,

Into the living sea of waking dreams,

Where there is neither sense of life nor joys,

But the vast shipwreck of my life's esteems;

And even the dearest—that I loved the best—

Are strange—nay, rather stranger than the rest.

I long for scenes where man has never trod;

A place where woman never smiled or wept;

There to abide with my Creator, GOD,

And sleep as I in childhood sweetly slept:

Untroubling and untroubled where I lie;

The grass below—above the vaulted sky.

NON SUM QUALIS ERAM BONAE SUB REGNO CYNARAE

Last night, ah, yesternight, betwixt her lips and mine
There fell thy shadow, Cynara! thy breath was shed
Upon my soul between the kisses and the wine;
And I was desolate and sick of an old passion,
Yea, I was desolate and bowed my head:
I have been faithful to thee, Cynara! in my fashion.

All night upon mine heart I felt her warm heart beat,
Night-long within mine arms in love and sleep she lay;
Surely the kisses of her bought red mouth were sweet;
But I was desolate and sick of an old passion,
When I awoke and found the dawn was gray:
I have been faithful to thee, Cynara! in my fashion.

I have forgot much, Cynara! gone with the wind,
Flung roses, roses riotously with the throng,
Dancing, to put thy pale, lost lilies out of mind;
But I was desolate and sick of an old passion,
Yea, all the time, because the dance was long:
I have been faithful to thee, Cynara! in my fashion.

I cried for madder music and for stronger wine,
But when the feast is finished and the lamps expire,
Then falls thy shadow, Cynara! the night is thine;
And I am desolate and sick of an old passion,
Yea, hungry for the lips of my desire:
I have been faithful to thee, Cynara ... in my fashion.

www.ingramcontent.com/pod-product-compliance
Lightning Source LLC
Chambersburg PA
CBHW011845200326
41597CB00028B/4713